# Blowout Sax

## A revolutionary approach to playing the Saxophone

"If music be the food of love, play on." William Shakespeare

# Blowout Sax

## A revolutionary approach to playing the Saxophone

### Mark Archer

Consultant
Craig Crofton

ISBN: 978-1-78003-857-5

Published by

# Blowout Sax

South Lodge, North Parade, Bath BA2 4EU
Telephone 07866 766133
Email blowoutsax@blowoutsax.com
www.blowoutsax.com

Published in 2009

© Mark Archer 2009

The right of Mark Archer to be identified as the author of this work has been asserted by him in accordance with the Copyright, Designs and Patents Act, 1997.

This book is sold subject to the condition that it shall not, by way of trade or otherwise, be lent, resold, hired out, or otherwise circulated without the publisher's prior consent in any form of binding or cover other than that in which it is published and without a similar condition including this condition being imposed on the subsequent purchaser.

The publisher is grateful to the following organisations for allowing their copyright material to be reproduced in this book:

### Music Sales Limited
*Bring Me Sunshine* (Dee/Kent) International Music Network/Campbell Connelly
*The Girl From Ipanema* (Gimbel/Jobim) Universal MCA/Windswept Pacific
*When I'm 64* (Lennon/McCartney) Northern
*Baker Street* (Rafferty) Universal

### Harmony Music Limited
*The First Time Ever I Saw Your Face* (MacColl)

### Warner Chappell and IMP (reproduced by permission of IMP Ltd)
*When I Fall In Love* (Heyman/Young) Warner/Chappell
*The Pink Panther* (Mancini) Warner Bros
*What A Wonderful World* (Weiss and Weiss) Valando Music Inc/Abilene Music Inc, USA/CarlinCorp
*Careless Whisper* (Michael/Ridgeley) Morrison Leahy Music Ltd

# Contents

| | |
|---|---|
| Acknowledgements | 8 |
| | |
| **Chapter 1** | |
| **Introducing the Dream Machine** | |
| Introduction | 11 |
| Types of Sax | 16 |
| Putting It Together | 18 |
| Mouthpieces & Reeds | 22 |
| Breathing | 24 |
| Embouchure | 28 |
| Touch Tight | 30 |
| The Illegal Key | 31 |
| The Naturals | 32 |
| The First Note | 33 |
| Middle C | 34 |
| Left Hand   B | 36 |
| Left Hand   A | 37 |
| Left Hand   G | 38 |
| Left Hand Dominant | 39 |
| Tone | 40 |
| Use a Mirror | 42 |
| Right Hand | 43 |
| Right Hand   F | 45 |
| Right Hand   E | 46 |
| Right Hand   D | 47 |
| Bottom C | 48 |
| Take a Break | 49 |
| Lower Register Naturals | 50 |

| | |
|---|---|
| The Octave Key | 54 |
| Upper Register | 56 |
| Upper Register Naturals | 58 |
| The Naturals | 60 |
| Working the Fingers | 61 |
| Play Every Day | 63 |
| The Dream Machine | 65 |
| | |
| **Chapter 2** | |
| **Glorious Opening Tunes** | |
| Introduction | 67 |
| Tonguing | 68 |
| Staccato | 68 |
| Legato | 70 |
| Legato and Slurring | 71 |
| Crossing the Bridge | 72 |
| 1st Tune: *Camptown Races* | 74 |
| 2nd Tune: *Ain't No Sunshine* | 79 |
| 3rd Tune: *Swing Low, Sweet Chariot* | 85 |
| 4th Tune: *When the Saints Go Marchin' In* | 88 |
| Learn a Tune by Heart | 90 |
| | |
| **Chapter 3** | |
| **Sing through Your Sax** | |
| Introduction | 93 |
| Sharps & Flats | 94 |
| F Sharp | 95 |

# Contents

5th Tune: *When I Fall In Love*    97
Wah-Wahs    100
Woo-Woos    102
Vibrato    103
6th Tune: *The First Time Ever I Saw Your Face*    106
C Sharp    110
7th Tune: *Careless Whisper*    112

## Chapter 4
### A Bluesy Interlude
Introduction    117
B Blues    118
8th Tune: *St James Infirmary*    121
9th Tune: *Mourning Blues*    124
Growling    Flutter Tonguing    126
Growling    Buzz    127
Growling    Kicker    128

## Chapter 5
### Two Little Fingers & B Flat
Introduction    131
G Sharp    132
10th Tune: *Brahms' Lullaby*    133
D Sharp    136
11th Tune: *John Brown's Body*    138
B Flat    140
12th Tune: *House of the Rising Sun*    142
Four Sharps & B Flat    145
Befriend the Keys    148

## Chapter 6
### Very Bottom Notes
Introduction    151
Bottom C    152
1st Tune Revisited: *Camptown Races*    154
13th Tune: *Pop Goes the Weasel*    156
14th Tune: *What a Wonderful World*    158
Bottom C Sharp    162
Bottom B    163
8th Tune Revisited: *St James Infirmary*    164
Bottom B Flat    165
15th Tune: *Nobody Knows the Trouble I've Seen*    166
Very Bottom Notes    170

## Chapter 7
### Very Top Notes
Introduction    173
Top D    174
16th Tune: *Baker Street*    176
4th Tune Revisited: *When the Saints Go Marchin' In*    179
Top D Sharp    181
Top E    182
3rd and 2nd Tunes Revisited: *Swing Low* and *Ain't No Sunshine*    184
17th Tune: *Amazing Grace*    185
Top F    188
18th Tune: *Yesterday*    190

# Contents

| | |
|---|---|
| Quick Top F | 193 |
| Quick Top E | 194 |
| 33rd Note: F Sharp | 195 |
| Very Top Notes | 198 |

**Chapter 8**
**The Chromatics**

| | |
|---|---|
| Introduction | 201 |
| Up and Down the Ladder | 202 |
| The Main Chromatic Notes | 204 |
| Learn It By Heart | 206 |
| 19th Tune: *Pink Panther* | 208 |
| 20th Tune: *Bring Me Sunshine* | 210 |
| 21st Tune: *When I'm Sixty Four* | 212 |
| 22nd Tune: *Girl from Ipanema* | 214 |
| 23rd Tune: *The Entertainer* | 219 |
| The Full Chromatic Scale | 224 |

**Chapter 9**
**The Finale Challenge**

| | |
|---|---|
| Introduction | 227 |
| 24th Tune: *The Can-Can* | 229 |
| 25th Tune: *In the Bleak Mid-Winter* | 237 |

**Chapter 10**
**You & Sax Mastery**

| | |
|---|---|
| Introduction | 243 |
| You | 244 |
| Be Yourself | 245 |
| Mouthpieces | 246 |
| Reeds | 248 |
| Experiment | 249 |
| Love Your Saxophone | 250 |
| Blowout Sax Scales Charts | 251 |
|    Tenor and Soprano | 254 |
|    Alto | 255 |
| *Blowout Sax Madmen* | 256 |
| *Blowout Saxology* | 256 |
| Improving Tone | 259 |
| *Blowout Blue Sax* | 261 |
| Pop Sax | 262 |
| Sax Kings of Jamaica | 264 |
| A Helping Hand | 267 |
| Favourite Tunes | 268 |
| Your Journey | 270 |
| You | 271 |
| We Did It | 272 |
| | |
| Bibliography | 274 |
| CD index | 276 |

# 8 ACKNOWLEDGEMENTS

## Acknowledgements

Hey Pops we did it, finally found the one! What a great, fun journey together . . .

Without the love of my life Cate who has encouraged me to new personal boundaries I never new existed. And for providing me with three brilliant sons, those colourful characters that are Belouis, Oscar Bonar and Beaujan.

Me mum for my life skills and flamboyance of character.

All the black and white photos by me top big broth', Simon Archer. And never to forget the lunatic big broth Paul who

# ACKNOWLEDGEMENTS

once played the Will You song, latently installing the desire to want to play the sax.

Me top inspirational mates . . . Moosh, Widgey, Age, Boggy, Dowie, Al-Boy, Colin, Ray, Prof, BTM.

My Blowout Sax compatriot teachers Stan, Berry, Rachel and Jackie.

To all those who have been through Blowout Sax in the last 20 years, a massive thank you for all your support on this musical journey.

Thanks to all the cartoon work by Ben Cook.

Original graphics of the sax by Michael Heyward.

Nearly all the black and white photos by Simon Archer, also thanks to Scott Morrison and Abbo snapshots in 'N'awlins'.

Original book draft help from Simon Walker and Andre Balkham and the man who revamped and patiently helped us over the finishing line, Tim Jollands.

The help, knowledge and record collection of dj and friend, Tony Clark.

The guidance of that instigator, William Pennington.

Thanks to my much lamented partner in music, Stevie D.

The top mixing and ear skills of Chris Cornish and Benji Bartlett who determinedly drove these recordings to a final conclusion – Huge Thanxs me B.

And finally, to Craig 'The Raj' Crofton who was cajoled into my own personal mission which was to write and rewrite this book, thank you again me pal.

*Mark Archer, January 2009*

# 10

"Music isn't the property of any one class, any one race, any one person."
Keith Richards

*chapter one*

# Introducing the Dream Machine

I am a self-taught saxophonist and over the past 20 years I've devised a revolutionary, fun and easy way of learning to play the sax. We use it to teach students at the Blowout Sax Schools.

# CH 1 – INTRODUCTION

My way is simple to learn and you don't need to have any knowledge of music theory.

This unique and proven method has been successfully taught to every age, profession, creed and colour.

This is *our* aim!

Every saxophone teacher has a different approach and I've proved mine works, as several of my students have been accepted into music college and many are up and playing with bands.

# Ch 1 – Introduction

Our method has been devised to get you blowing well, as quickly as possible. You will develop and improve as you progress through the book.

Some folk believe they lack a musical ear but, people do have one. You'll learn to listen properly. The sax is the instrument that will allow you to explore your musicality *by training your ear.*

Our specialised approach is ideal if the sax is your first instrument. If you've been formally taught any instrument, ignore any previous methods, because this is unlike any musical approach you've come across before.

## CH 1 – INTRODUCTION

Some of the greatest musicians – Bob Dylan, Sting, Ray Charles, David Bowie and Van Morrison (a decent sax man) – have been seduced by a desire to play the saxophone. Even the late great John Lennon blew some outlandish tenor sax on *Helter Skelter*.

The saxophone is the *Dream Machine*. It has beauty, style, with a sound so human and magnificent, and yet so moody and sad. **It is the most exciting and versatile instrument.** Yet like the majority of instruments it's taught in a very dull and sterile way.

# CH 1 – INTRODUCTION

The aim is to smash the myth that playing the sax is difficult and to remove the shroud of secrecy that surrounds it. In my experience this route has opened doors to non-music readers and has allowed them to learn and succeed in playing, this instrument of dreams.

# Ch 1 – Types of Sax

There are two principle types of saxophone to learn on, the alto and the tenor.

The **alto** has a bright, very adaptable tone and it is comfortable for anyone who is young or of small to medium height.

Alto

Tenor

The **tenor** has a rich deep tone which needs lots of air and is much larger and heavier than the Alto. It has a lower range and also sounds great.

# CH 1 – TYPES OF SAX

Choose the one that you fancy playing and don't be swayed. But play the size of the sax that suits you. I've noticed through the years that in general, if you're 6 foot plus and well built, you'll be comfortable playing the more physical tenor. However if you are smaller, then the alto is for you.

Most importantly, get a good sax (see page 22), a decent ligature, a known make of reed and a top sling. It is 80 per cent of your future.

I wouldn't start on the **soprano**, the straight one . . .

. . . or the enormous **baritone**. Try these later, as they are awkward to start on, despite having the same principles of playing.

# CH 1 – PUTTING IT TOGETHER

Now let's put the sax together.

Take the main **body** of the instrument.

Take the part of the neck called the **crook**.

Loosen the **screw** at the top of the horn and then twist the crook into the top of the main body. Make sure the crook is overlapping the little **rod**, at the back.

# Ch 1 – Putting It Together    *19*

Set the crook up so it is more or less straight in line with the bell end. Tighten the screw at the top of the horn.

Now let's put the **mouthpiece** together. For the time being, use the basic plastic one that comes with the sax.

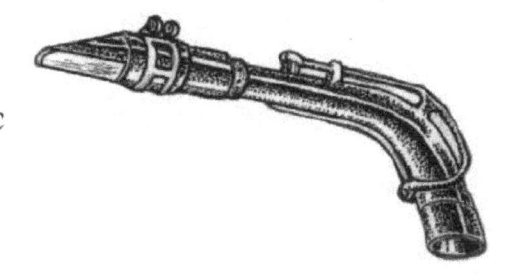

Start with a 1½ Rico cane **reed** if you are under 15 and 2 or 2½ if you are an adult. Lick the reed on both sides and always soak a new reed for about 10 minutes as you need a moist reed to get a good sound.

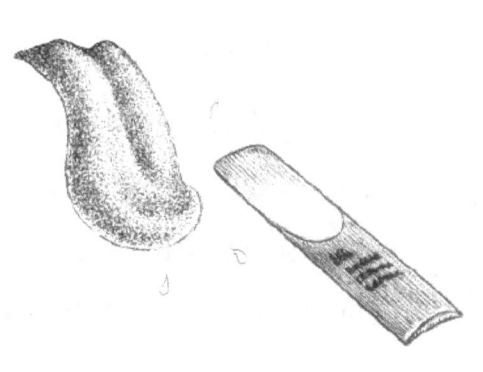

# Ch 1 – Putting It Together

❶ Place the reed on the mouthpiece, with the curve of the reed just below the tip of the mouthpiece. ❷ Take the **ligature**, which is the metal or leather attachment, and slide it over the reed and mouthpiece.

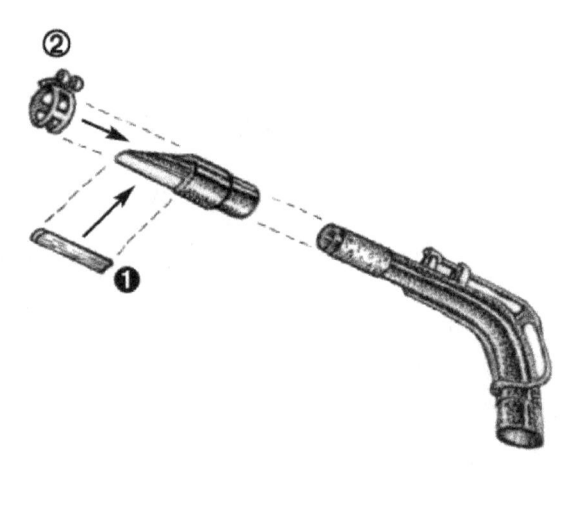

Beware tearing the reed when sliding the ligature down the mouthpiece. Tighten the 'lig' so it's tight but not too tight. Make sure that it fastens the reed so it does not move. Then screw the mouthpiece about 80% of the way down the cork.

This will **tune** your saxophone. If you are playing along with our CD use your ear to check if it sounds in tune. Sometimes when your sax is too hot or cold you may have to move the mouthpiece up (to make it flat) or down (to make it sharper) until the tuning is right. Mark the position with a pen so you can find it again.

# CH 1 – PUTTING IT TOGETHER

Then clip the **sling** on the back of the sax. We recommend a padded and elasticated Neotech sling to ease the weight of the sax and to keep it balanced. It's worth having a padded strap as a cheap one will tug at your neck. Put the strap over your head and place your left thumb on the black circle. Put your right hand thumb under the **hook**.

Pull the strap up so the mouthpiece goes straight into your mouth. Don't lean your head forward, let the mouthpiece come to you so it feels comfortable, your head is straight and you are set up nearly ready to start blowing.

# Ch 1 – Mouthpieces & Reeds

Before you start blowing, though, you must understand what makes up your sound. Your sound will be unique. If you lined up 30 horn players and asked them to play the same note, each would sound wildly different. Why? Here comes the gospel of sound.

The answer is that *four different elements make up your sound*. The first two are the **saxophone** itself and the **mouthpiece/reed**. Each sax has its own feel and personality. The make and price vary. Usually the more expensive the better, especially the French, American and Japanese ones.

Nowadays **mouthpieces** are quite varied and can be made from rubber, metal, glass and ebonite. Often the basic mouthpieces that come with the sax are incredibly difficult to blow.

# Ch 1 – Mouthpieces & Reeds

---

### The Reed Strength Guide

| 1, 1½, 2 | 2½, 3 | 3½, 4 |
|---|---|---|
| **LIGHTWEIGHT** | **MIDDLEWEIGHT** | **HEAVYWEIGHT** |
| *thin, easy to blow* | *warm sound* | *thick, harder to blow* |

---

If this is the case, lash out and buy a Selmer C*, Rico Royal or Yamaha mouthpiece. These are relatively cheap, easy to blow and give a very pleasant sound. Having the most basic mouthpiece on your sax is like buying a Mercedes with a gearstick that doesn't work.

On your mouthpiece, your **reed** makes a big difference to your sound. You'll start at a number 1½ or 2 Rico reed and as your jaw and lip strength builds up, you'll try half a reed size up. The thicker the reed, the richer your sound. So if you change both the horn and the mouthpiece/reed you change half your sound. *Keep your reed moist.*

# Ch 1 – Breathing

Take care too that you're not too clumsy with the reed as you take the horn out of your mouth. Tears have been shed on reeds ripping on jumpers and jackets through absent-mindedness.

What really makes you sound different to everyone else are the last two elements of **breathing** and your facial features, which we poshly call the **embouchure**. Learning to breathe properly is absolutely crucial. A guitar sounds when strummed, a piano sounds when touched, yet a sax without air is silent.

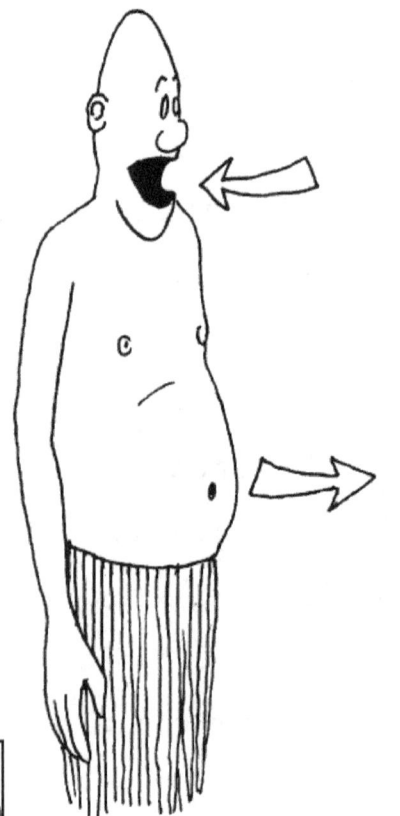

Now when you see your Doc and he asks you to breathe in, normally you inhale and push your tum inward. *Totally wrong.* For your whole life your haven't been breathing properly. What a revelation!

# CH 1 – BREATHING

When you draw in air to blow the sax, at the same time push and *keep pushing the stomach out*, right from your guts while blowing out. This is the way to breathe properly.

Watch someone in a deep sleep, and see them breath correctly. So the general idea is as if you're trying to show your friends how large your belly is, or you're watching a child unload in their underwear! The foundation is your guts which will give you your wind!

Try to breath properly before you start blowing the sax. Keep your cheeks tight while blowing out. Bring the air from your guts and you'll be wonderfully surprised how much wind you've got. Breathing through your stomach will help give you the body of an athlete while doing something you really enjoy!

# Ch 1 – Breathing

To get used to breathing, lie on the floor, put a book on your tum and inhale at the same time. Push the book upwards while blowing out and hold the book in the air for as long as possible.

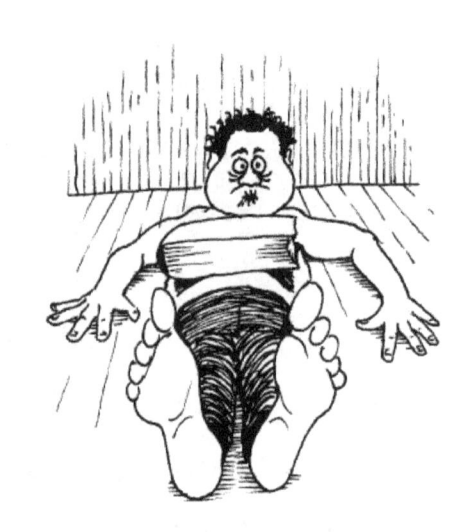

So when you take air in, keep pushing out with your stomach. If you don't, you may feel very wobbly, dizzy and fuzzy in your head, as though you had a Scotch too early in the day. So basically, you now know how to breathe.

Also while breathing, be aware of keeping an *open throat*. Air can stop in the throat if you are feeling stressed or wound up. Remember when you were in trouble at school, you would

# Ch 1 – Breathing

gulp air like mad. This cuts off the air, so be supremely relaxed and the throat will stay open and the air can pass through easily.

The sax is like being with a loved one. If you are happy and laid back it goes fine. But if you are tense, nothing works. Remember this whenever you play.

You'll be more aware of your breathing at the early stages and then after a short while it will become second nature. Breathing has to be mastered because it is generating your sound.

# Ch 1 – Embouchure

*Sound The Fanfare!* The moment has arrived to get a note out. The final crucial element is the **embouchure** (em-bou-chure). The embouchure is your facial features, chin, cheeks and lips, and these play a huge role in shaping your sound.

Now consciously remembering your new discovery in life, how to breathe, rest your two front teeth on the top of the mouthpiece. This holds the mouthpiece steady and stops it sliding around. *Don't bite*, just let it rest.

Put the mouthpiece in your mouth about a third of the way in, and slightly curl your bottom lip over your bottom teeth, so it acts like a cushion for the reed. Don't bite the reed because it doesn't taste at all pleasant.

# CH 1 – EMBOUCHURE

Never bite your bottom teeth into your bottom lip – never ever! One geezer I taught told me that he couldn't get a sound out of it as he believed you had to bite your bottom teeth into your bottom lip to produce a sound. All he got was bleeding gums and a whine. That is one horribly false and kinky concept.

The three fingers of the left hand are always covering all three keys even when they are not being pressed down. Left thumb rests on back **thumb rest**. Try to just touch the tips of the keys, not cover the whole of them, as this will help with

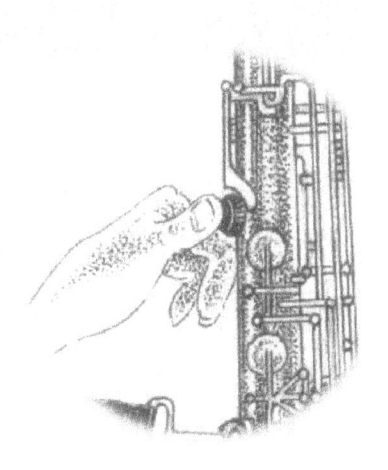

# CH 1 – TOUCH TIGHT

hand speed later. The right hand does exactly the same, with the right thumb under the thumb rest.

Make sure you are holding the sax away from your body and ensure you are standing up straight so you are not slouching or leaning forward into it. The mouthpiece should almost be level as it can really affect your sound. *Back straight, head straight and don't be lazy.* Hold the sax out either to the front or to one side.

The fingers need to be *touch tight* to the keys no matter what note you are playing.

# CH 1 – THE ILLEGAL KEY

Beware touching the **illegal key** at the top of the neck, marked by an 'X' – see page 36 for exactly where this is.

Had a geezer call me after buying a sax.
"I can't get a note out," he screamed frantically.
"Are you holding down the illegal key at the top?" I replied.

## Problem solved.

I suggest putting some sticky tape or Bluetak on the illegal key, so you know when you are accidentally touching it.

## Ch 1 – The Naturals

Now we introduce

# the naturals

The names of the notes go from **A** to **G**: **A**, **B**, **C**, **D**, **E**, **F**, **G**. There is no note **Q**, **T** or **Z** but it's a wacko idea. We call these notes the **naturals** – all the white keys on a piano.

So, starting with the thumb on the back thumb rest, the first note to blow is **C**. Only use the second finger of the left hand, to depress the key as shown on page 34. Curl the left hand around the top keys and make sure you do not touch them (see photo on page 30). Bend and lift the left hand so it looks as if you are limp-wristed.

Keep your bottom lip relaxed and add just a little pressure to the reed. Make sure your top and bottom lips are in alignment (see page 28). Now, without touching any other

# Ch 1 – The First Note

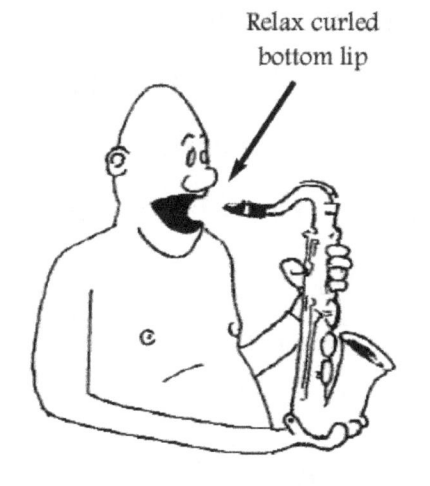

Relax curled bottom lip

keys, push the sax away from the body.

Check that the two front teeth are just resting, bottom lip relaxed, tongue out of mischief resting at the bottom of the mouth, gulp and push out with the stomach and blow, keeping the lips level, to form a seal – that is, not smiling. Sound at last!

Now you are looking for the **sweet spot**, so move your mouthpiece in or out of your mouth a little to hear it sounding 'sweet'. You may notice the note is a bit on the wobbly side. So when you blow, keep the air nice and steady and centre it straight into the mouthpiece. Blow a long steady note with a sweet tone.

# Ch 1 – Middle C

**① C**

Really listen to track 1 on the CD. Really sing the note, hum it, play it in tune, play long notes – get it into your head. The aim is to know how every note sounds by heart. Because if you can 'hear' a note before playing it, or intuitively can find it – that is an ultimate goal of a saxophonist.

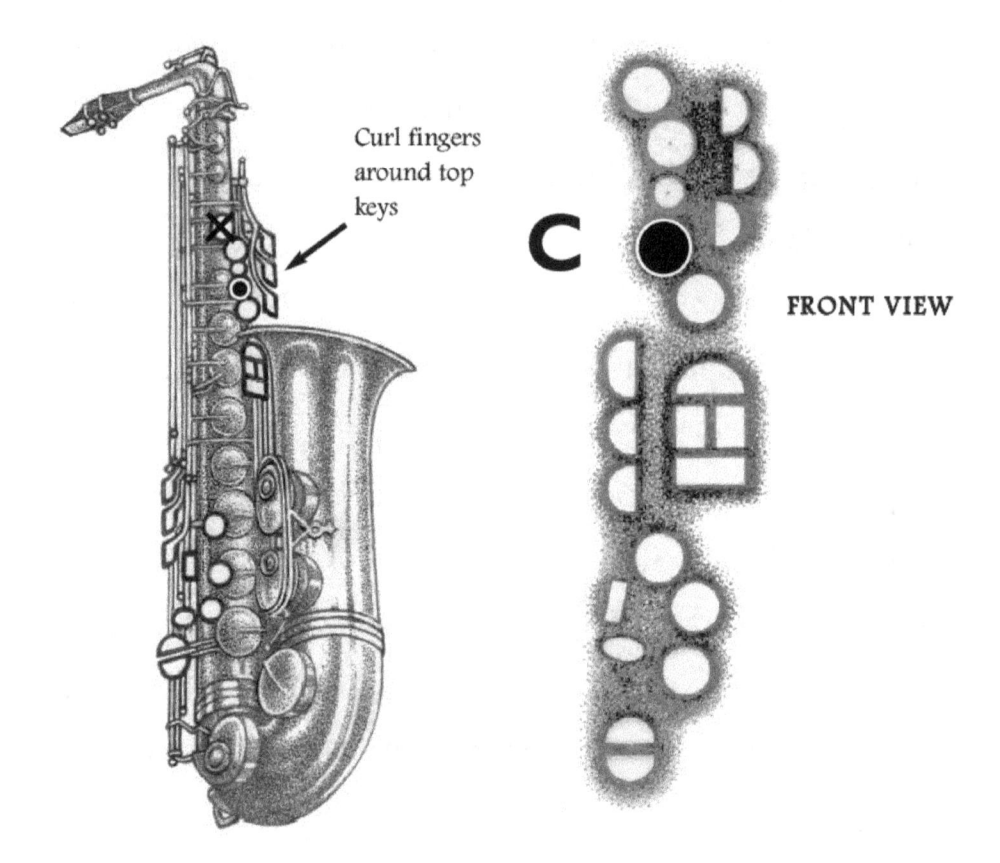

Curl fingers around top keys

C

**FRONT VIEW**

# Ch 1 – Middle C

So breathing low from your tum/guts, cheeks tight, blow **C** again. Make sure it is in tune with the CD – if it's not, tighten the muscles of your mouth.

Blow softly through the mouthpiece. Keep your lips towards the tip. Keep the sound of each note steady. Keep your cheeks tight and relax your bottom lip.

If you feel like you don't have enough wind, try this style of breathing – the **Active Gulp**. What you do is rest the two front teeth on the mouthpiece and drop the bottom jaw and gulp air deeply, at the same time keeping your stomach pushed out.

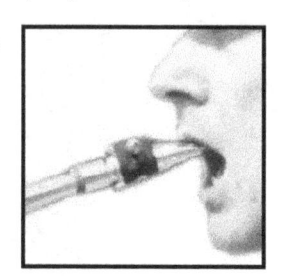

This is a billion times more useful than setting your embouchure and then just using the air inside your body. Because when you're blowing, that isn't an awful lot of air. You look like a goldfish, scoring few points for cred, but it really works! So drop the jaw and **actively gulp** the air in

# CH 1 – LEFT HAND – B

**(2)** B

Now using the first finger of the left hand play **B**. Be careful with the **B** not to just touch the **illegal** key.

**(3)** C to B 'The Switch'

Once you've got this sounding sweet, alternate playing between **C** and **B**. I call this **The Switch**. Blow gently and softly back and forth, **C ⟷ B**. This is the hardest manoeuvre we will make until Chapter 2 so practise it.

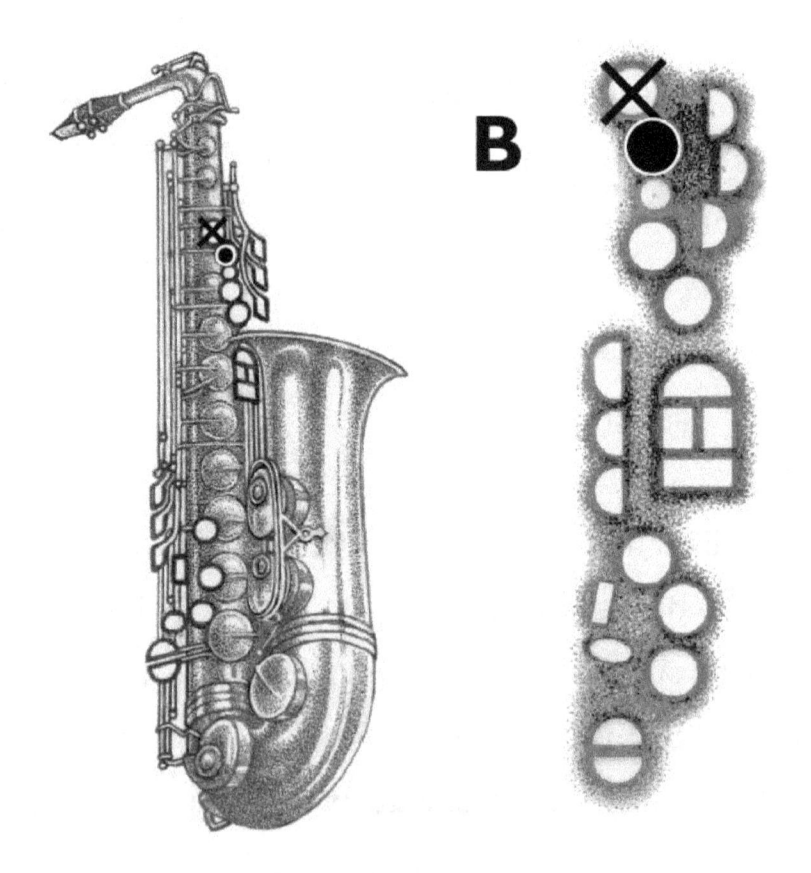

B

# CH 1 – LEFT HAND – A

## 37

Next, the **A**. Press the top two keys together like those legends Winston Churchill, John Lennon and Harvey Smith.

( 4 )
A

Now alternate the three notes: **C** ⟷ **B** ⟷ **A**. Slowly, carefully and softly. There's no point in knackering yourself 'parping' like a demented demon. Blow every note and hold it steady for a good 10 to 15 seconds. Play long notes.

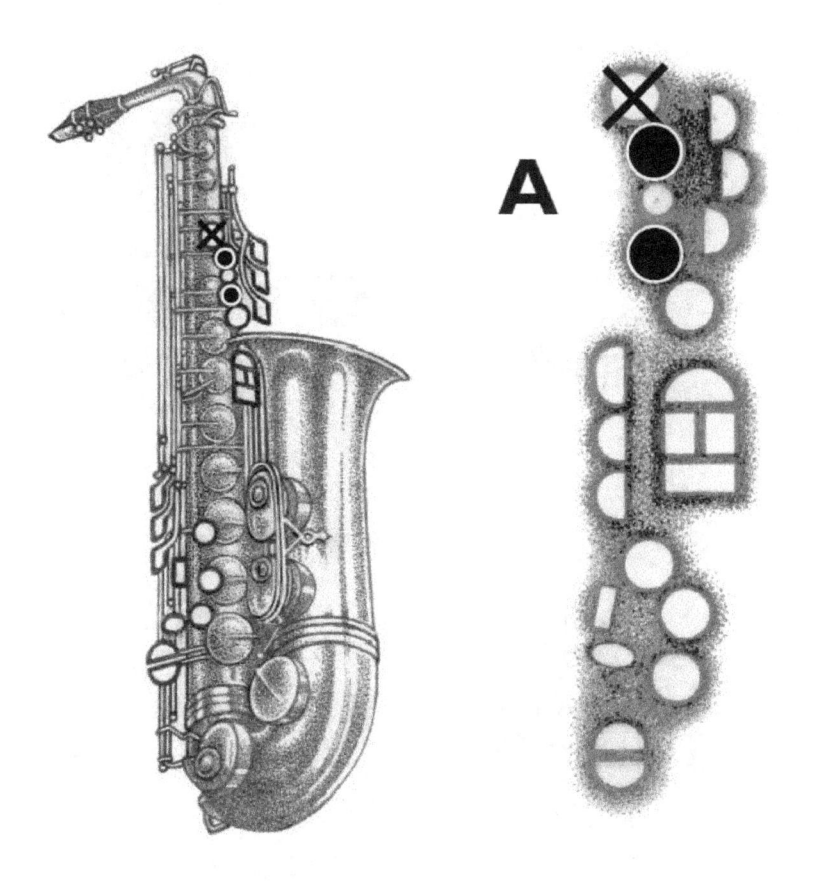

A

# 38  CH 1 – LEFT HAND – G

(5) G

Now to complete the left hand, with three keys pressed down, here is **G**.

Accommodate the **G** key by bending your ring finger slightly more than the other two.

Always use **G** to tune to as it's mid-range on the sax.

# CH 1 – LEFT HAND DOMINANT

The sax is left-hand dominant. When I started, all my left hand did was, while driving, change gears, hold down paper while writing and wear Russian wedding rings. Yet suddenly, it needs to retrain itself real quick. The left hand does become skilful over a period of time, and takes the *main role*. If you are left-handed you are a real lucky rascal, and you should thank your lucky stars.

So you will learn to breathe properly and be ambidextrous – supple up those fingers for lots of uses!

# Ch 1 – Tone

If you are having problems getting a nice sound/tone then here are a few things to check.

1. Make sure the reed is moist and is on the mouthpiece properly (see page 19). This will affect your sound/tone.

2. Check fingers are in the right place (see page 30).

3. Should a sound not be coming out, check that your bottom lip is relaxed and not pressing too heavily against the reed. The reed must be allowed to vibrate freely. Blow again. If once again there's no joy, slide the mouth a tiny bit further down the mouthpiece. Find your sweet spot.

Sound we will call **tone**. The golden rule is, *the softer you blow, the better the tone.* Also, try to keep your embouchure as relaxed as possible. The more the reed can vibrate naturally, the sweeter the tone. So relax the bottom lip and focus in on just putting enough air in to get the sax blowing.

# Ch 1 – Tone

Now if you blow as hard as possible, it sounds harsh, a honking sound. So readjust the mouth further towards the tip and blow softer. You don't have to blow very hard to get a sound. The sound of the sax carries over two miles away with wind assistance. I know because in the South of France I once blew, quietly of course, and the folks on the beach could still hear my sexy tone.

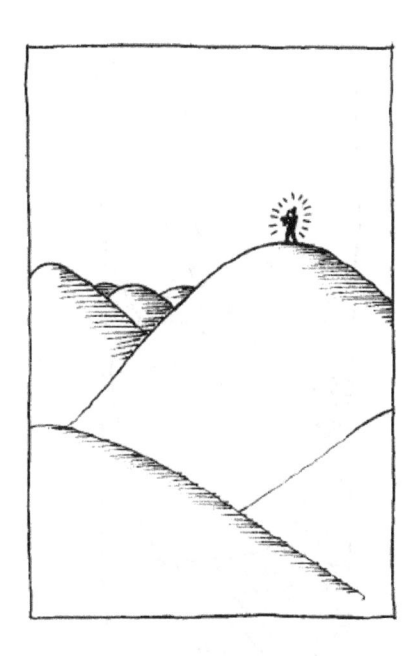

Keep your cheeks tight and never puff them. If you are puffing them, the air isn't getting to your guts, and that's where you want your air to come from.

You may see good sax players puffing their cheeks out, but start off with tight cheeks. If you want to practise getting your cheeks together, try whistling and then smiling broadly. Or blowing through a straw without puffing out your cheeks.

## Ch 1 – Use a Mirror

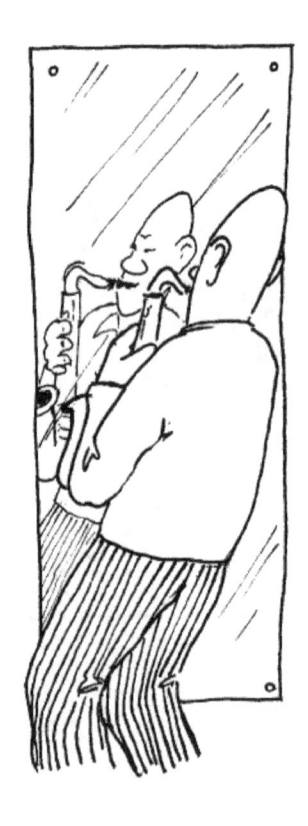

Do this repeatedly, but not while driving – one of my punters was stopped by coppers at a set of traffic lights while strengthening her embouchure in this way and nearly got carted off to the loony bin!

Now, whenever you play your saxophone, put yourself in front of a full length mirror. This technique is named after Narcissus the Greek, who loved looking at himself. This is the way to check your breathing, embouchure and soon, your fingers. It's a great habit to cultivate. You can check out what you are doing, and correct any naughty habits.

Folk will call you extremely vain when they see you doing this, but it does work. The mirror acts as your teacher to guide you.

# Ch 1 – Right Hand

So far the right hand has been *'Bone Idle'* and in the early stages you will **never** use the right hand unless your left hand has *all three fingers down*. The right hand, up to now, has just had a *supporting role*. Now curl the right hand around the side keys. Place the tips of your fingers over the keys so they are *touch tight*. And don't forget about your right thumb underneath the thumb rest.

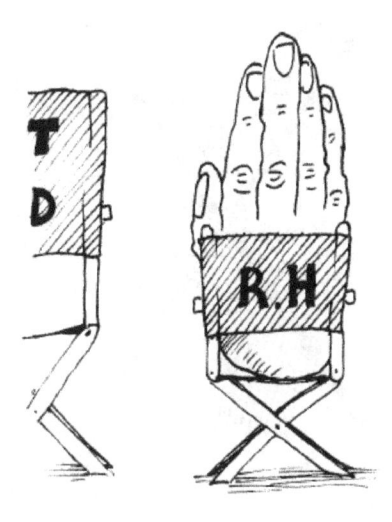

The awesome Charlie *'Bird'* Parker use to skin-up Jamaican Woodbines with his right hand while playing with his left. This is wonderful flamboyance, but you get the general idea. Store up all this arrogance for *later*.

Keep the right hand poised and ready, sitting on the pearl keys. It's useful to practise in front of the mirror watching your hand positions, so there isn't a *taxi journey* to the keys.

# Ch 1 – Right Hand

You will **never** put the right hand down on the keys unless the left hand has **all three fingers** pressed down (until later . . . ).

Now let's introduce the right hand into our *'organised mayhem'*. For these lower natural notes, the trick is – whether you have been playing for 12 minutes or for 96 years – to **blow really softly** and **push out from the stomach**. If a note ever squeaks, relax your bottom lip a little.

# Ch 1 – Right Hand – F

**45**

Next the **F**.

⑥
F

Put the first finger of the right hand on the first pearl key. Lift the right hand over the side keys, just touching the tip of the keys. Adjust the right hand thumb under the hook, until the fingers are *touch tight*.

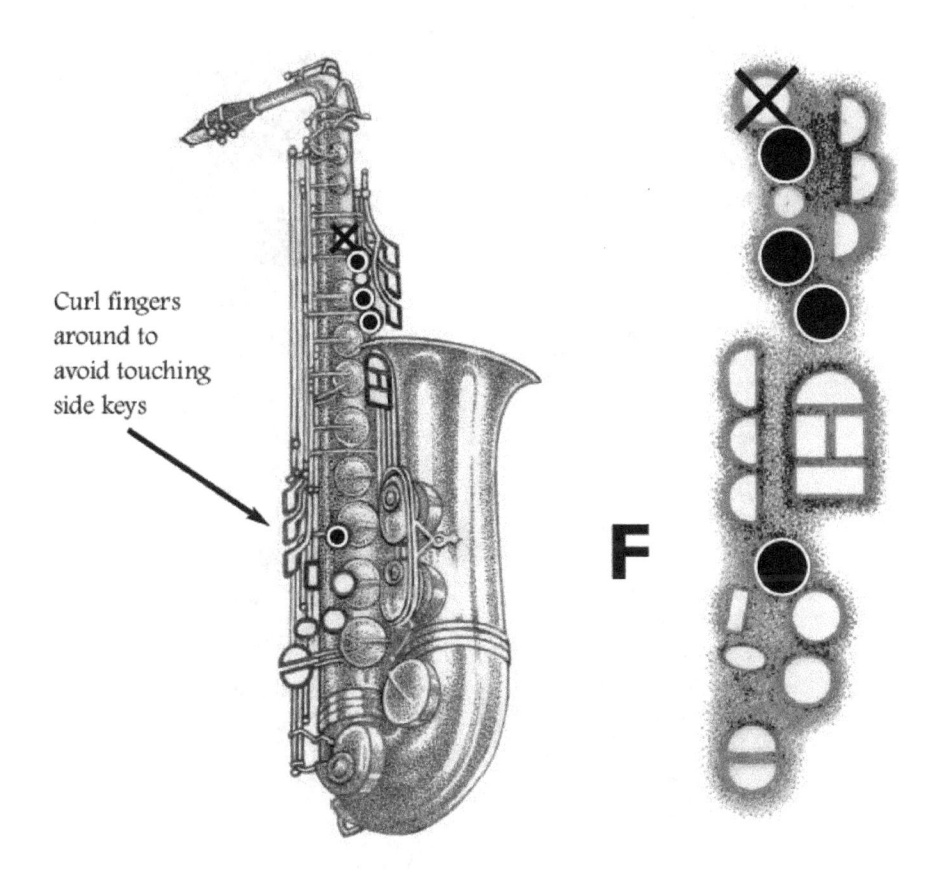

Curl fingers around to avoid touching side keys

**F**

# Ch 1 – Right Hand – E

**(7 E)**

Next the **E**, now using two fingers of the right hand.

Make sure the notes are low. If they come out too high make sure you are not overblowing – i.e. blowing too hard and fast. Keep them *low, deep* and *sexy*. **Think low...** also, relax the bottom lip/embouchure to allow the reed to purr.

**E**

# Ch 1 – Right Hand – D

Finally, here's **D**. With the third finger of the right hand, this completes the seventh natural. Push from the guts. *Stay relaxed!* Think **tone:** *what does it sound like?* Remember, loosen your bottom lip and embouchure just a little. Be careful with this note – the sax is an imperfect instrument (which is why we like it) but it can be flat. Check the tuning with the CD.

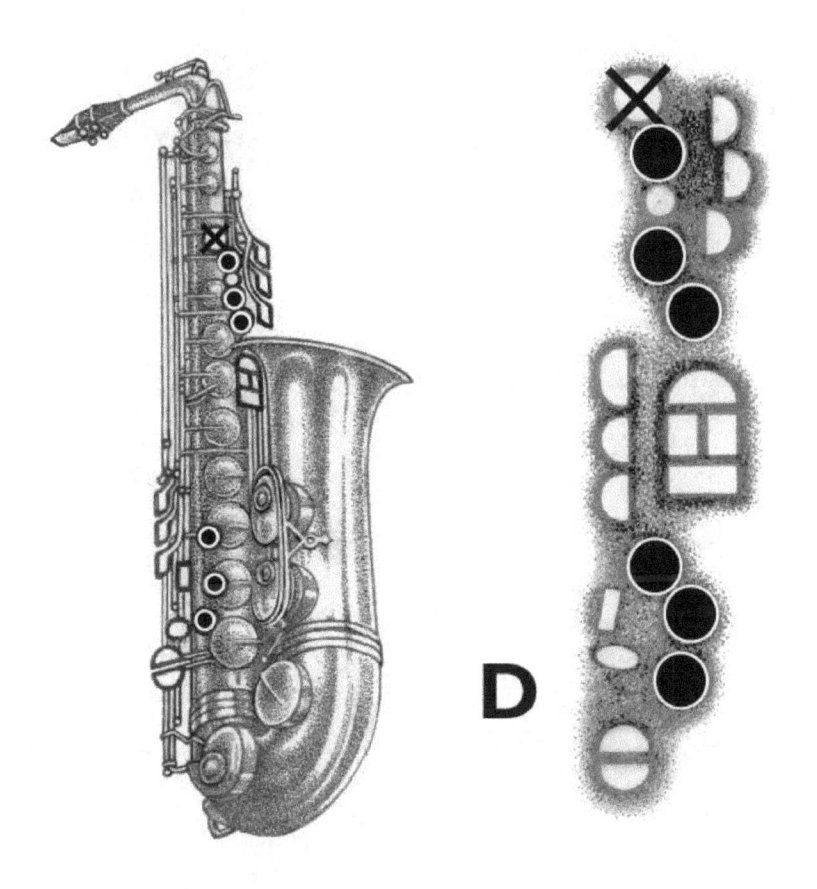

**D**

# Ch 1 – Bottom C

**(9) botC**

Now try **bottom C** (botC). To get this note out, relax bottom lip – **think low** – if it doesn't come out immediately, take in a little more mouthpiece and honk it out.

Now try running down to botC from **F** in one breath: **F-E-D-botC**.

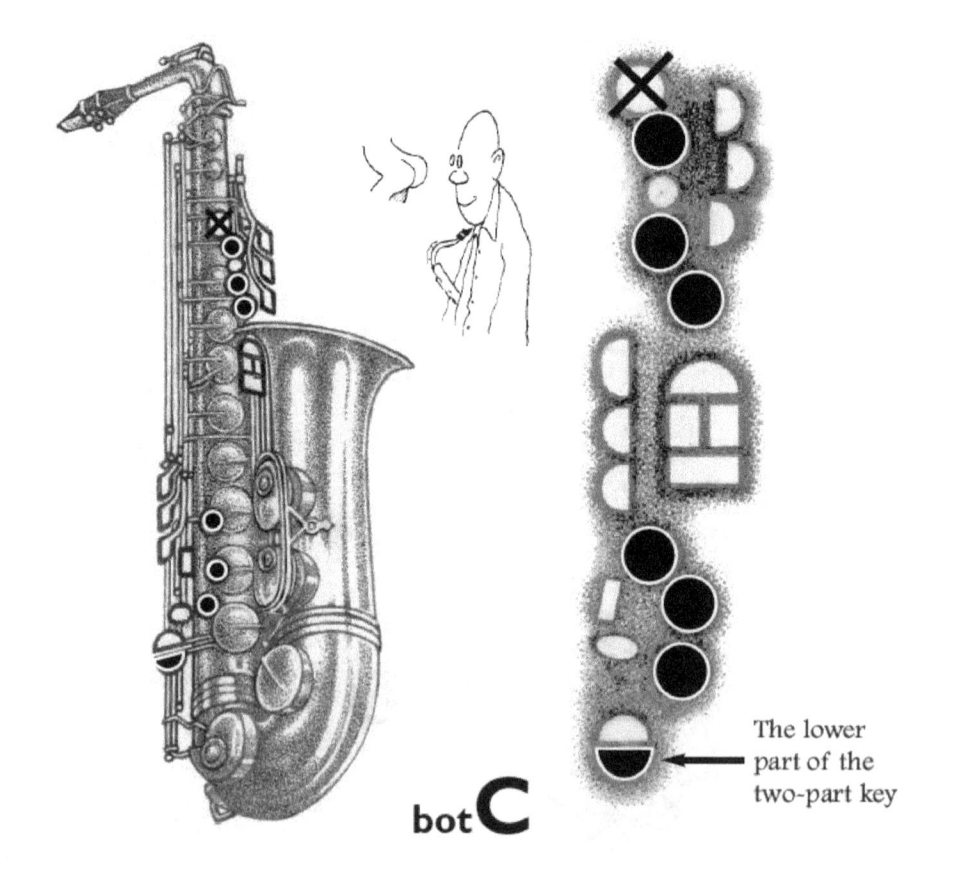

bot**C**

The lower part of the two-part key

# CH 1 – TAKE A BREAK

Now after about 10 to 15 minutes stop. I said stop!! **Stop!!!** Let the cheek, chin and lip muscles build up because unless you have been grinning like The Joker for about 3000 years they won't have the strength.

Have a break and then have another go. I had an overenthusiastic bloke who went on hols with his newly purchased sax. He overworshipped it and played for an hour and a half straight, day and night. By the end of the week his bottom lip had ballooned up and he couldn't blow for ages. Would you go to a gym and do the heaviest weights for hours, not having done them before?

So build up the time spent playing, up to 20/25 minutes on a daily basis, and then have a blow again. Again, it's like a loved one: it will give you grief if you don't show it enough attention and that applies however long you've been playing! The strength of your embouchure builds up really quickly.

# CH 1 – LOWER REGISTER NATURALS

**10**
C B A G
F E D botC

So now we have sorted out **C-B-A-G-F-E-D-botC**, all with the octave key **off**. Eight notes – we're cooking! This is called one **octave**. If you want to remember the order, think: **(C)-BAG-FED** – see **(C)** like a horse feeding **(FED)** out of a nosebag **(BAG)**.

This is also the first of a dozen major scales used for jamming – **C major**. Now play all the notes blowing continuously, running the fingers down. Now try running the fingers back up: botC-D-E-F-G-A-B-C. Remember when you start blowing the **D** to **think low** and blow softer than you think. Do it in one breath.

**11**
botC D E F
G A B C

At the top end, between the **B** and the **C**, remember **The Switch** is the other way round.

# CH 1 – LOWER REGISTER NATURALS  *51*

**C major**

bot **C D E F G A B C**

**Arpeggio**

bot **C E G B C**

*52*

*Left Hand*

C  B  A  G

*Octave Key* **off**

C  B  A  G

# Lower Register Naturals 8/33

**FED**

53

C/BAG/FED

**F**  **E**  **D**  bot **C**

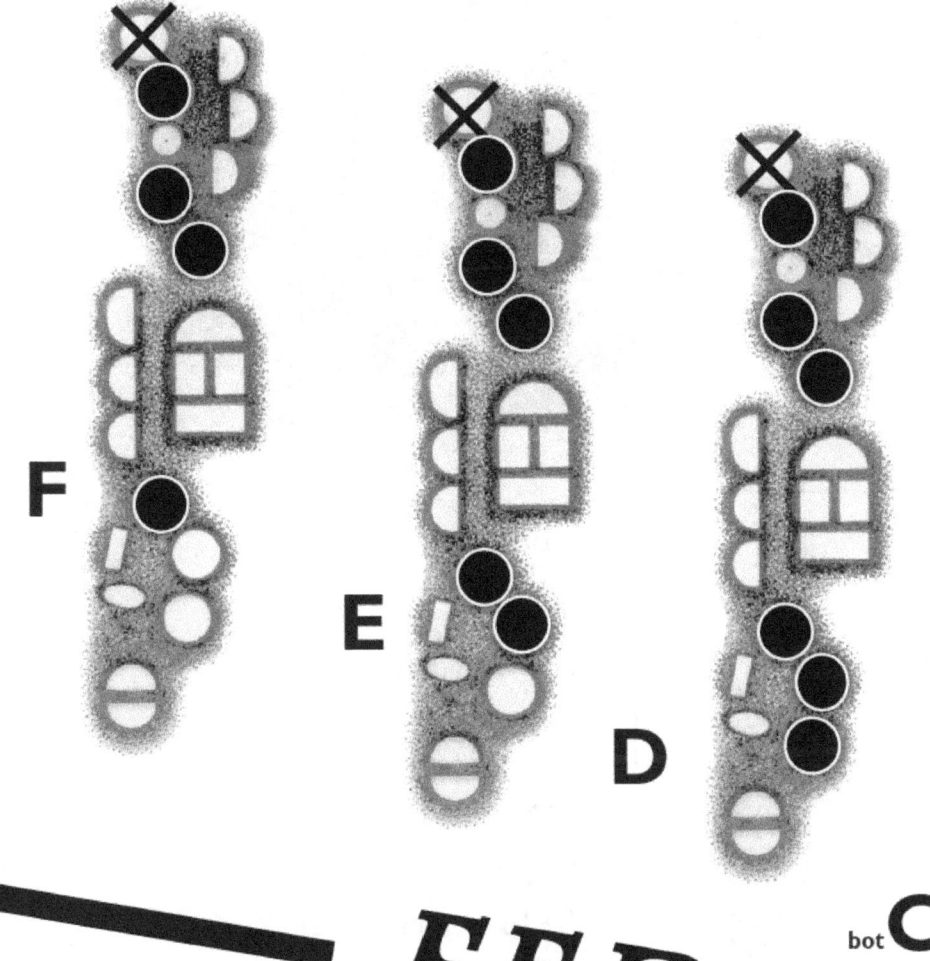

**FED**

Right Hand

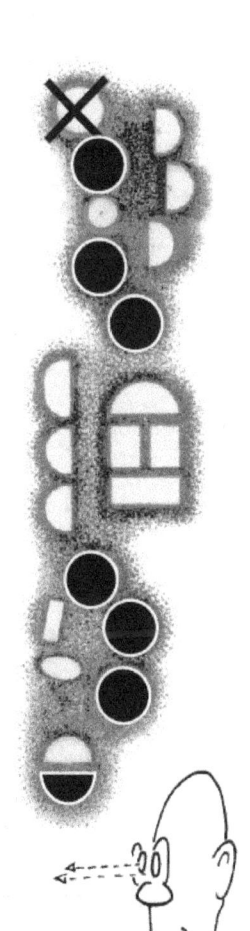

# Ch 1 – The Octave Key

The sax is split into two registers, divided by a key at the back called the **octave key** where your left thumb WILL sit just below it on the black thumb rest.

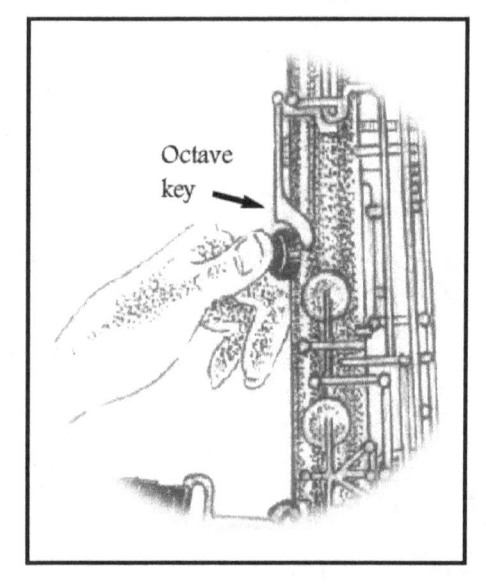

When the O.K. (as it is casually called) is pressed **down** you are in the upper register (high/treble) and when it is not you are playing the **lower register** (low/bass).

# CH 1 – THE OCTAVE KEY

It's easy to remember – think of your *moods*:

(on) = **HIGH**

off = **LOW**

# CH 1 – UPPER REGISTER

The good thing is when 'Our Father' Adolph Sax created this instrument 150 plus years ago, he made the *fingering position* on the keys for the naturals exactly the same whether the thumb was (**on**) or **off**. The only difference in notes is one set is high and one set is **low**. So now you have learnt the fingering of the natural notes for one register, it is the same for the other – **excellent!**

**12** (D)
**13** (E)
**14** (F)
**15** (G)

There are **33** notes on the sax and we've already looked at the lower register first (see pages 52-53). Now let's double our notes from **8** to **15**, using the (upper register), pressing the octave key *down* with the left thumb. We are now (**on**).

Start playing (D) – all six fingers down and run them into the (E), (F) and (G). If your (G) *'grumbles'* you are swallowing a little too much mouthpiece. Move your mouth

# CH 1 – UPPER REGISTER

a tiny bit towards the tip. The note should now sound clean and pure. If the sound sometimes gets husky, suck your spit back in!

For the (**A**), (**B**) and (**C**), **slightly** tighten your **bottom lip**, blow a bit faster and **think high**. Make sure each note sounds in tune by playing the same note with the octave key **off**. *Let your ear be the judge*, listening hard to make sure it sounds **perfect**. Always check with the recorded notes on the CD.

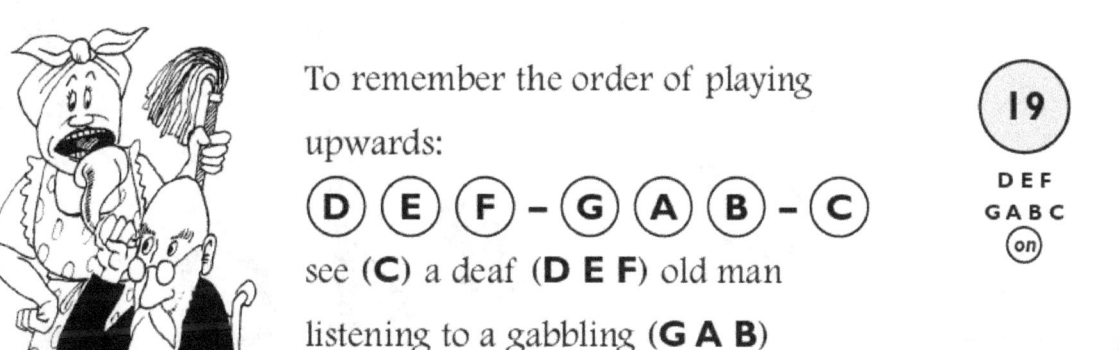

To remember the order of playing upwards:

(**D**) (**E**) (**F**) - (**G**) (**A**) (**B**) - (**C**)

see (**C**) a deaf (**D E F**) old man listening to a gabbling (**G A B**) blabbermouthed ole boot. Playing the notes up and down in the upper register, *'upstairs'*, is a little easier than with the thumb **off**, *'downstairs'*.

16 (A)

17 (B)

18 (C)

19
D E F
G A B C
(on)

# 58

## C  B A G

**Left Hand**

Octave Key **on**

C   B   A   G

## C  B A G

DEF/GAB/C

# Upper Register 15/33 Naturals

**FED**

C/BAG/FED

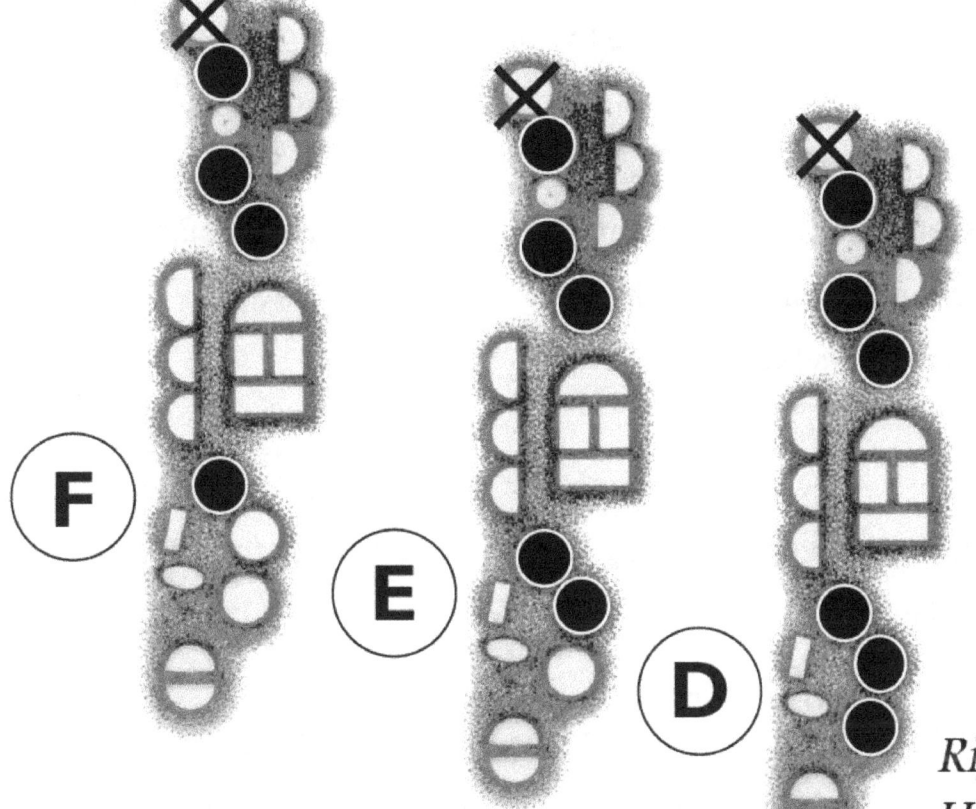

**FED**

Right Hand

# Ch 1 – The Naturals

Now you have **15** notes called *'the naturals'*. You will use these as the **mainstay** of your playing throughout your sax career – day in, day out. Really **think** the notes when you're playing them, i.e. in your head. The sax can do anything *you* want it to do. All you have to do is **think it**.

You are now in the sax roadshow. If you can blow those sweetly you'll already sound **impressive**. Learn the name of each note by heart. All the *upper register naturals* are grouped together for you on pages 58 and 59.

Now you've got the hang of the natural notes, there are a number of cunning ways for the fingers to *befriend* the keys.

The next time you are relaxing in front of the goggle-box, try this. Without blowing, take the whole sax, including the crook, just press the keys up and down playing legitimate, normal, natural notes – **no** wacko fingerings, please.

# Ch 1 – Working the Fingers

The closing of the pads will sound like you are lightly playing the notes. This is the way to *acquaint* your finger positioning and yourself with the keys.

Getting the fingers working right is about a quarter of the game. Let your fingers feel at home.

# CH 1 – WORKING THE FINGERS

I once taught a poseur who was a lifeguard. He did this non-stop for eight hours a day by the pool and boy did his fingers move quickly! This shows your fingers and the keys can become great maties and is also a useful pastime for when your *'chops'* have gone!

Also don't forget Narcissistic learning. That full length mirror is your self-corrective teacher. It's the ultimate way to check fingers, active breathing and that your bottom lip is relaxed.

---

### Chapter 1
*Introducing the Dream Machine*
**Summary**
• We have learned 15 natural notes

*Things to remember*

• Finger positions, Reeds, Embouchure, Breathing

---

# Ch 1 – Play Every Day

It is my law to make every single saxophonist buy a stand. Set the sax up and place it on the stand somewhere prominent. It is beautiful to the eye and every time you pack it up to go out make sure you set it up the moment you come back. This only takes a minute. This way you can pick it up at a moment's notice and have a session. Otherwise it will stay hidden. Now your beauty is on display and entices and seduces you to blow your saxophone. Remember to carefully replace the protective cap over the mouthpiece when you're not playing.

Watch where you place the stand. If you place it somewhere too prominent then this can lead to disaster. Another punter was indulging in some carnal knowledge and unfortunately an outstretched leg kicked the saxophone, smashing it to pieces. The moral of the story is have the stand somewhere prominent but safe and away from radiators.

Play your sax every day. The saxophonists who do this are the most successful ones. Play every morning when you get up. Stay in love with your shapely beauty.

# CH 1 – PLAY EVERY DAY

If you stop playing for more than a week it acts like a neglected lover, all sore and angry. The *'chops'* – your lip and jaw strength – won't last too long initially, but the sax soon forgives and lets you both in.

At the early stages, explain to your family and friends that there'll be a few difficult weeks but promise the glorious day when you'll be playing fluently will come quickly, especially as you'll be using my fantastic method of learning. Actually ask for support.

Don't overload on information. The next day, check that you really do know what you've learned the day before. Use the mnemonics and hilarious cartoons to help you remember.

# Ch 1 – The Dream Machine

So be patient and prepare to escape into your own world. Encouragement from your family and friends is important, but at the end of the day, be confident. With every play you will become more intimate with your sax.

Keep that dream alive. Playing is a great adventure, some days exhilarating, when you are truly touching paradise. Other days it just ain't there. But keep trying for a few minutes, as often you can groove into the mood.

It is addictive, escapist and when you are switched on and hooked that stays with you forever.

"I don't know anything about music. In my line you don't need to." Elvis Presley

## chapter two

# Glorious Opening Tunes

**B**efore we put those Natural notes into songs we have to learn two very important aspects of playing the sax. The first of these is

*the art of tonguing*

# Ch 2 – Tonguing

The tongue is the most important primary colour and is vital to brighten up your playing. So, how to tongue when playing the sax. This took me far too long to master, and it will take you about 30 seconds!

Blow the note **C** (octave key **off**) and hold it for about 10 seconds and at the end of this time lift your tongue and place it on the reed. The result – *the note stops dead.* Now blow for five seconds, and lift the tongue to touch the reed. Again the note stops dead. Try for one second, then add the tongue so the note immediately stops. That's it! You are now tonguing. These short, crisp notes are called **staccato.**

Now to refine **staccato,** without blowing, say "T" and practise flicking the tongue out of your mouth almost as though you have a slight lisp.

**20**
'T' Staccato on a **C**

So, blow the **C**, say "T.T...T.T..." flicking the tongue on and off the reed. The note should be short. You are aiming to flick the tip of the tongue on the tip of the reed. The 'T' should just

# CH 2 – STACCATO

**tickle** the end of your tongue at the start of the note, and should sound soft, light and clipped. Make sure you are holding the sax away from your body, standing up straight. The mouthpiece should be level. It is best illustrated by a dot over the note: •

The aim is to coordinate the tongue with the fingers. The way to do this is to play the **staccato** on all the natural notes, with one 'T' for each note. Try **C major**:

**C B A G F E D** bot**C**

As you will hear, use **staccato** like a *spice* in your cooking – just a little to give it taste but not too much or you'll have *Montezuma's revenge!* At the other extreme, none at all and the music will be bland.

---

21

C B A G
F E D bot C

Staccato

# CH 2 – LEGATO

Knowing how to play **staccato** leads to the other important form of tonguing.

**Legato** is flicking the tongue on and off at the beginning of **C** (octave key **off**) together with blowing through the rest of the note. So, what we have is one continuous long note, with the tongue flicked on and off at the start. This is best illustrated by a ·— . Try this in **C major**:

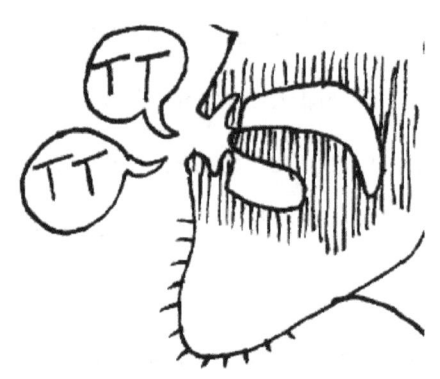

**C B A G F E D** bot**C**

The difference between these two tonguing methods is that **legato** is a long note with a highlighted beginning and **staccato** is just a short clipped note.

Keep the tip of the tongue on the tip of the reed so that it has a soft and subtle effect on the note. It should just

# Ch 2 – Legato and Slurring

touch and make one clean sound. If it makes two sounds then you are not getting the tongue off the reed quickly enough. Remember, keep the sax away from your body standing to attention. Mouthpiece level.

Try the **legato** on every note. Then try it on every second note. Then on every third, fourth, fifth and sixth notes. Really listen to the different ways this affects your phrasing. Using the tongue in this way really brings certain notes alive, and keeps each phrase interesting.

Last but not least, **slurring** is when you blow and move the fingers up and down changing from one note to another smoothly without tonguing. Since you started playing, this is what you have been doing – *'let those fingers do the walking'.*

**23** Swing feel tonguing every other note

**24** Swing feel tonguing every 3rd note

**25** Swing feel tonguing every 4th note

**26** Swing feel tonguing every 5th note

**27** Swing feel tonguing every 6th note

**28** Slurring
C B A G
F E D bot C

# Crossing the Bridge

This is the second aspect of playing that we need to learn before putting those naturals into songs.

*'Crossing the Bridge'* is moving from **C** up to **D** (six fingers) while depressing the octave key at exactly the same time. Get used to crossing the bridge back and forth with no hesitation or stopping to admire the view. It seems like an awful lot of work to move only one natural note, from **C** to **D**, but this is the way Adolf designed his saxophone and it becomes second nature with time.

Remember a **D** will take slightly more air than a **C**. Think of it as a seamless journey from one register to another.

# CH 2 – CROSSING THE BRIDGE

73

Make sure your fingers are *touch tight* to the keys and remember the left-hand thumb should be sitting **over** the octave key. If one finger or thumb is even fractionally late arriving at the keys, the note will sound distorted. Work on these hand movements until you can cross the bridge smoothly – this is exactly the sort of finger exercise you can do in front of the TV.

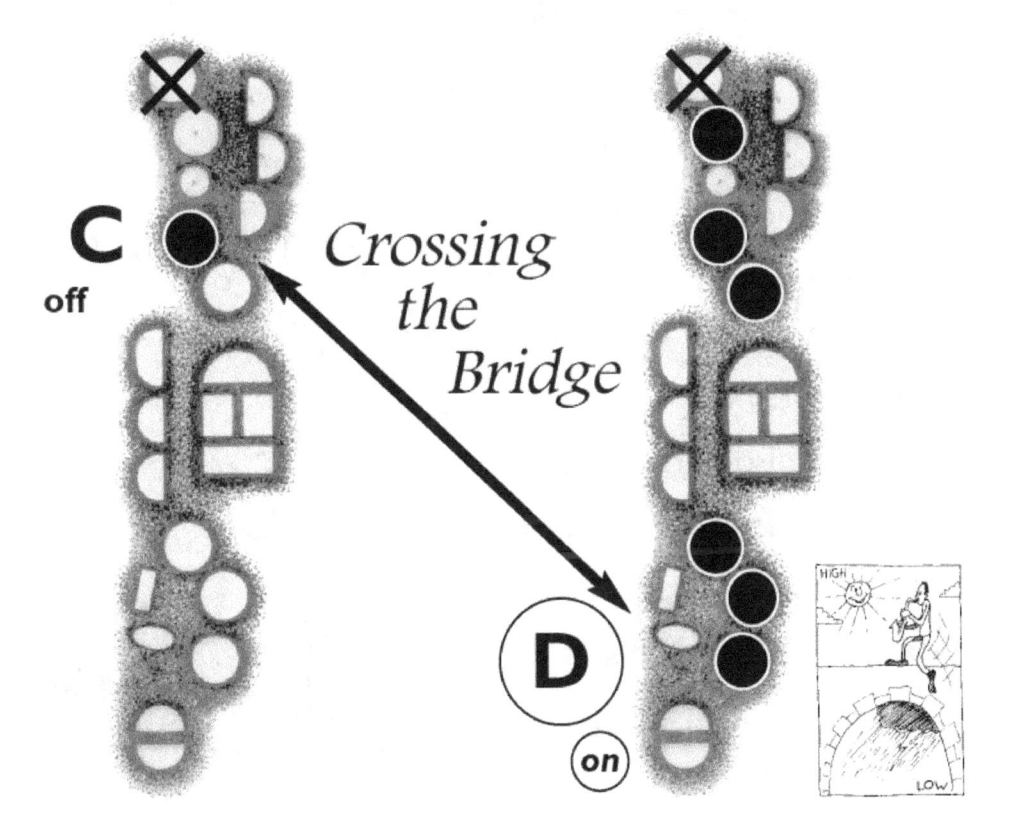

**C** off

*Crossing the Bridge*

**D** on

29

Crossing the Bridge
C to D

# Camptown Races
### Foster (1850)

The best way to start coordinating the left and right hand natural notes is to play lots of tunes. This will enable you to feel confident with playing around with the order of the notes you've just learned. Then you can really start showing off.

This one is free. Cost me 'nought pence'! I liked that and the ridiculous in me kept hearing the cartoon rooster 'Foghorn Leghorn' singing it. And Camptown also starred in one of the opening send-up gags penned by Richard Pryor in Mel Brooks's *Blazing Saddles* with 'them Yankee cowboys'. To cap its immense cred, I stumbled upon a random

# CAMPTOWN RACES

two-minute version by one of my favourite alto saxmen, Paul Desmond, originator of the most famous jazz-pop crossover, *Take Five*, with his famous accomplice, pianist Dave Brubeck.

Over the page is the layout of the notes for *Camptown Races*, split into phrases. All you need to do is to play the notes in the order they are laid out, breathing where shown. Listen to the CD. Octave key **(on)**.

All tunes are split up into musical **Phrases**. A musical phrase is just like a spoken sentence. Sometimes we say short phrases, *'yeah…I dunno'*, and sometimes we gabble on for hours before drawing breath. A musical phrase, just like a verbal one, starts and finishes upon breathing, the words being replaced by notes. Remember the saxophone is an extension of your singing voice.

# CH 2 – 1st Tune

## *Camptown Races*

Verse 1 Camp-town la- dies sing that song / ²Doo-dah Doo-dah/

**(30) Slow with sax**

Ⓖ  Ⓖ Ⓔ Ⓖ Ⓐ Ⓖ Ⓔ /  Ⓔ Ⓓ Ⓔ Ⓓ /

³Camp-town race track five miles long/

Ⓖ  Ⓖ Ⓔ  Ⓖ  Ⓐ Ⓔ /

**(31) Slow without sax**

⁴Oh! De-doo-dah day! /

Ⓓ Ⓕ Ⓔ Ⓓ C /

Chorus ⁵Gwine to run all night! / ⁶Gwine to run all day! /

C  c Ⓔ Ⓖ Ⓒ /  Ⓐ  Ⓐ Ⓒ Ⓐ Ⓖ /

⁷I'll bet my mon-ey on de bob-tail nag /

Ⓖ Ⓖ Ⓔ  Ⓖ  Ⓐ Ⓖ Ⓔ /

⁸Some-bod- y bet on de bay. /

Ⓓ  Ⓕ Ⓔ Ⓓ  C /

Listen to me playing the tune on the CD. Really get your inner ear listening to music as proactively as possible because this whole approach is about listening by ear, which is crucial. You have to really have big ears to learn about this instrument. *Camptown Races* – play the phrases very, very slowly indeed on their own.

# Camptown Races

## 77

## *Camptown Races*

Verse 2  ⁹I came down dah wid my hat caved in/ ¹⁰Doo-dah Doo-dah/
Ⓖ Ⓖ Ⓔ Ⓖ  Ⓐ Ⓖ Ⓔ/ Ⓔ Ⓓ Ⓔ Ⓓ/

¹¹I go back home wid a pocket full of tin /
Ⓖ Ⓖ Ⓔ Ⓖ Ⓐ Ⓖ   Ⓔ /

¹²Oh! De Doo-dah day! /
Ⓓ   Ⓕ Ⓔ Ⓓ Ⓒ /

Chorus  ¹³Gwine to run all night! / ¹⁴Gwine to run all day! /
Ⓒ Ⓒ Ⓔ Ⓖ Ⓒ / Ⓐ Ⓐ Ⓒ Ⓐ Ⓖ /

¹⁵I'll bet my mon-ey on de bob-tail nag /
Ⓖ Ⓖ Ⓔ Ⓖ Ⓐ Ⓖ Ⓔ /

¹⁶Some-bod- y bet on de bay./
Ⓓ   Ⓕ Ⓔ Ⓓ Ⓒ /

OK, so we are going to do a verse of *Camptown Races*, beautifully, slowly, with the music. Listen to it, get your ear going and once you feel confident try and play that along with me and along with the music. Once you have got that then try to do it on your own. But first things first, get it accurate, get it singing, and get it sounding beautiful.

# CH 2 – 1ST TUNE

The main fingering difficulty will be in phrases 5 and 13, when you cross the bridge from **C** with the octave key **off** to the (**E**) with the octave key (**on**), then to (**G**). From the (**G**) with three fingers you are then going to have to pivot to the high (**C**). That is going to be the main area of awkwardness, so get your fingers used to working and doing exactly what you are telling them to do.

The other thing, there will be two bridge crossings from the (**E**) to the (**D**), falling to the **C**. Now do this tune slowly, do it accurately, and get it sounding as beautiful as possible. Now try playing it on your own. Once you have got it accurate we will be speeding it up and doing a real cowboy showdown, *Blazing Saddles* version of it.

Finally, *Camptown Races* is in the key of **C major** (happy). Every song we play will be in a specific key. It is essential to play each scale as part of learning the songs. If you know the specific scale really well, the song you are playing will be so much easier.

# Ch 2 – 2nd Tune

# Ain't No Sunshine
## Bill Withers (1971)

One of the most soulful of songs is *Ain't No Sunshine*, by Bill Withers, whose version featured in the film, *Notting Hill*. It's a moving, top melody in the key of A minor (sad). For a mind-blowing version, seek out a recording of the late great Isaac Hayes's 17-minute epic at the Wattstax concert in 1972, when the 'Black Moses' spellbound his followers not only with 'that' voice but also with his alto saxman Emerson Able blowing some superlative sax phrases.

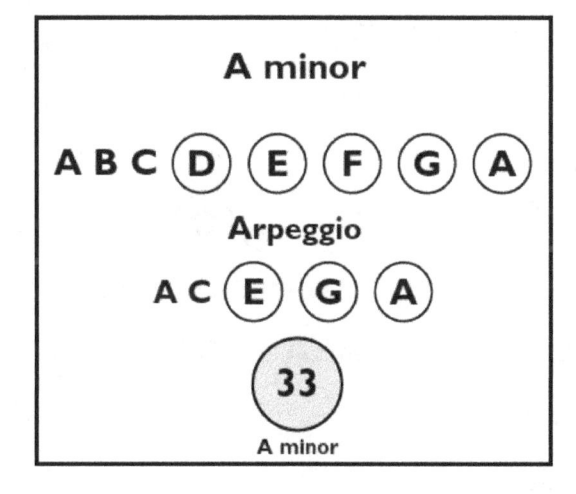

**A minor**

A B (D) (E) (F) (G) (A)

Arpeggio

A C (E) (G) (A)

(33)

A minor

## Ch 2 – 2nd Tune

### Ain't No Sunshine

Verse 1   [1]Ain't no sun-shine when she's gone /

**E   G  A   C      B   G   A** /

[2]It's not warm when she's a-way /

**E   G   A    C    B  G A** /

[3]Ain't no sun-shine when she's go- ne /

**A   A   C   (E)   (D)   (E)(E)(D)** /

[4]And she's al-ways gone too long /

**C   (D)   C   A    G    A    A** /

[5]An-y-time  /  [6]she goes a-way //

**C(D)C   /   A   G  A  A** //

Verse 2   [7]Wonder this time where she's gone /

**E   G  A   C      B   G   A** /

[8]Wonder if she's gone to stay /

**E   G A C   B  G A** /

[9]Ain't no sun-shine when she's go- ne /

**A   A   C   (E)   (D)   (E)(E)(D)** /

[10]And this house just ain't no home an-y-time /

**C   (D)   C    A   G   A  A    C(D)C** /

[11]She goes a-way //

**A   G  A A** //

# Ain't No Sunshine

81

## *Ain't No Sunshine*

Phrases 12-19    ¹²And I know, I know, I know,  I know       /
                   **E  GA    GA    GA    GA  C** /

                ¹³And I know, I know, I know,  I know       /
                   **E  GA    GA    GA    GA  E** /

} 12-13 x 4

²⁰Hey    I ought to leave young things a-lon-e  /
     **E  (D) (E) (E) G   (E)   D   C (D)**  /

²¹But ain't no  sun-shine when she's gone  /
      **ᴳ (E) (D) (D)  C    A    G   A**    /

Verse 3    ²²Ain't no sun-shine when she's gone  /
      **E  G  A  C   B   G   A**  /

²³On-ly dark-ness every day  /
     **E  G  A   C  B  A** /

²⁴Ain't no sun-shine when she's go- ne    /
     **A    A   C   (E)   (D)   (E)   (E) (D)** /

²⁵And this house just ain't no home an-y-time  /
     **C  (D)  C    A   G    A    A    C (D) C**  /

²⁶She goes a-way  //
     **A   G   A  A**  //

(cont.)

## Ch 2 – 2nd Tune

### *Ain't No Sunshine*

Verse 4  ²⁷Wonder this time where she's gone /

**E  G A C    B  G   A  /**

²⁸Wonder if she's gone to stay /

**E   G A C    B  G A /**

²⁹Ain't no sun-shine when she's go- ne /

**A   A  C   (E)   (D)   (E)(E)(D) /**

³⁰And this house just ain't no home an-y-time /

**C  (D)  C   A  G  A  A   C(D)C  /**

³¹She goes a-way / ³²An-y-time / ³³She goes a-way /

**A  G  A  A  /  C(D)C  /  A  G  A  A /**

³⁴An-y-time / ³⁵She goes a-way /

**C(D)C  /  A  G  A  A /**

³⁶An-y-time / ³⁷She goes a-way /

**C(D)C  /  A  G  A  A /**


Now as you can see there was a definite **C** to the (**D**) and back to the **C** so that is why there are bridge crossings. Any repeat notes use the tongue and, if you can, start thinking

## Ain't No Sunshine

about where you are going to introduce the legato, where you can flick the tongue on to make certain phrases count. Without the tongue it has got a completely different sound. So really think about where you are putting the tonguing and the legato within this tune. This is a song, like *Camptown*, that we will be coming back to later to do in a higher register.

Learn to play *Ain't No Sunshine* by heart, that is without looking at the notes. Once you've done this, try **stretching** the phrases, holding the notes longer and longer, playing really slowly. So you are working on improving your breathing and concentrating on pushing your stomach out. But don't go all wobbly.

Later on in your saxophone career, you will be blowing non-stop on certain tracks for up to six or seven minutes. So it is vital to breathe the correct way from the start.

# Ch 2 – 3rd Tune

# Swing Low, Sweet Chariot
## (traditional)

Living in a rugby crazed city, and with the Blowout Sax HQ positioned a big garryowen away from Bath's Recreation Ground, next up is *Swing Low, Sweet Chariot*. This presents you with an easy opening gig at the boozer or mate's gaffe for England's rugby internationals. I even taught this to the popular England and Bath rugby celebrity, Victor Ubogo.

The thing with *Swing Low, Sweet Chariot* is to practise pivoting, crossing the bridge from the (**D**) to **B** it's just a different bridge to the one from (**D**) to **C**, so coordinate the fingers accordingly: (**D**) ↔ **B**, **B** ↔ (**D**). Just practise that movement. The other bridge we're going to have to cross is from (**D**) to **G** – so again, slow the air down, keep the air as soft as possible as you cross the bridge. *Swing Low, Sweet*

## CH 2 – 3RD TUNE

*Chariot* we're now going to put on the music on and I'm going to do a little play along version. Again, this will be on your CD, listen to it, really get the tune in your head. Point the pen along with the fingering as well and really think about how I'm phrasing it and what I am putting in to produce the sound of *Swing Low, Sweet Chariot*.

Make sure that you have really got your fingers around each and every single phrase. Remember as you hit the low **D** to slightly slacken off a little bit with the jaw. Have your bridge crossing beautifully poised so there is no mistaking that you are getting it really smooth. Also remember to just tongue as you cross the bridge – so when you go from the (**D**) to the **B**, flick the tongue on legato style just to settle the note down. Same thing with the **G**.

First things first. Play the track solo, get it really accomplished, right under your fingers, and then have a go with the music in given time. Again, we will come back to this one – we're going to play it up high as well.

# Swing Low, Sweet Chariot

## 87

### *Swing Low, Sweet Chariot*

Chorus 1, 2 and 3

¹Swing low / ²sweet char-i- ot /

(D)  B  /  (D)  G  G ED /

³Com-in-g for to carry me home /

G G G G B (D) (D) (D) /

⁴Swing low / ⁵sweet chari-ot /

(E)(D)B /  (D)  G G ED /

⁶Com-ing for to carry me home /

G G G G B B  A G  /

Sequence
Chorus
Verse 1
Chorus
Verse 2
Chorus

**34** With sax

**35** Without sax

Verses 1 and 2

⁷I looked over Jor-dan / ⁸and what did I see /

B(D)G G G E G / G G G G E D /

⁹Com-in-g for to carry me home /

G G G G B (D)(D)(D) /

¹⁰A band of angels coming after me /

(D)(E)(D) B B/G G G E D /

¹¹Com-ing for to carry me home //

G  G G G B B  A G  //

CH 2 – 4TH TUNE

# When the Saints Go Marchin' In
### (traditional)

The fourth tune in this chapter is immortalised by that jazz legend, pop star, actor and global ambassador of goodwill, Louis 'Satchmo' Armstrong. Play *When the Saints* like this icon did – with wholesome joy. I make no apologies for teaching many of his favoured tracks because this man from New Orleans will always possess that magical ability to make us smile. As a musical pioneer he developed his own inimitable sound with an intensity and an expressiveness few can rival. That is the ultimate goal of a musician.

In this tune we are crossing the bridge often from **C** to (**D**). By now this should be seamless. The big thing is to get the bounce and the buoyancy and general joy. Use lots of staccato to keep the tune bright, driving on, and get it 'under your fingers'.

# When the Saints

**89**

Verses 1 and 2

¹Oh when the Saints /

**G B C Ⓓ /**

²Go mar-ching in /

**G B C Ⓓ /**

³Oh when the Saints go mar-ching in /

**G B C Ⓓ B G B A /**

⁴I wan-na be in that num-ber /

**B B A G G B Ⓓ Ⓓ C /**

⁵When the Saints go mar-ching in /

**B C Ⓓ B G A G /**

㊱ Verses 1 and 2 with sax

㊲ Verses 1 and 2 without sax

When you play this, or any other tune, let the melody run around in your head. Transfer the **feel** and the **rhythm** of this to the **touch** of your fingers. Hence the term *'dancing with your fingers'*.

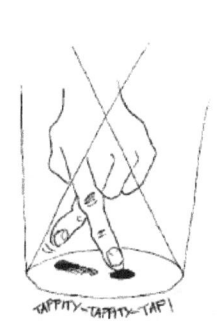

We'll go back to add higher verses to *Camptown* and *When the Saints* to help these opening tunes sing even more.

# CH 2 – LEARN A TUNE BY HEART

> **Chapter 2**
> *Glorious Opening Tunes*
> **Summary**
> We have learned:
> • Four famous tunes, two of which we'll come back to later
> • Crossing the Bridge smoothly
> • Tonguing so it highlights the notes
> • Getting those fingers coordinated
> The CD will reinforce the tunes and help us in
> • Developing Big Ears to learn to play along

We want you to learn each tune by heart and here's how:

1. Play the first phrase twice.

2. Turn the page over and then play it again. If you don't play it right, look for the note you are missing. This will help with note recognition in your brain – figure that out yourself. The more you do this the better you will get at it, to the point

# CH 2 – LEARN A TUNE BY HEART

where with me I can hit the note straight off – this is the way to becoming a good musician, especially playing by ear. Then with time you'll be able to work out any piece of music, even your own phrasing, really quickly.

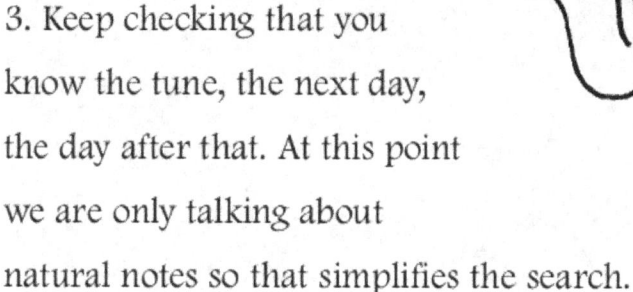

3. Keep checking that you know the tune, the next day, the day after that. At this point we are only talking about natural notes so that simplifies the search.

This is what we call having the tune 'under your fingers', so you can pick it up and show off at a moment's notice how good you already are on the saxophone.

"Learning music by reading is like making love by mail." *Isaac Stern*

# chapter three

# Sing through your Sax

Learning to read music can freak you out! Some of the most successful musicians couldn't read: Lennon & McCartney, Louis 'Satchmo' Armstrong, Jimi Hendrix and countless others. Don't flip out at the names of the notes in this chapter – they are **easy** to play.

# Ch 3 – Sharps & Flats

The saxophone is about feeling, passion and joy so don't get hung up about reading the dots. You won't have this anxiety because, as you know, your *innovative* authors have worked out this special approach to sidestep that colossal headache.

Until now, we've been learning the white notes on a piano. Now we're going to add the **black notes**. We call all of these notes *Sharps* with the exception of one, which is a flat. Each note is a bit schizophrenic and has two names. **F** sharp (written **F#**) can also be called **G** flat (written **G♭**). It's a bit like folks spelling a name Mar<u>c</u> or Mar<u>k</u>. It doesn't make a blind bit of difference. So sharps are half a note **up** from the named note and flats are half a note *down*.

# Ch 3 – F Sharp

95

Now to check out these new notes, with five new sets of fingerings – the first is **F#** (also known as **G♭**).

( 38 )
F#

First, ensure your left thumb is **off** the octave key, and the three fingers of your left hand are on the first three keys. Now add the second finger of your right hand. This is your *'tickler'* or *'road rage'* digit.

**F# / G♭**

# Ch 3 – F Sharp

A good way to remember the name of this note is to think of cutting your finger on a *sharp* knife. You would curse saying "that's *FFF . . . ing sharp*".

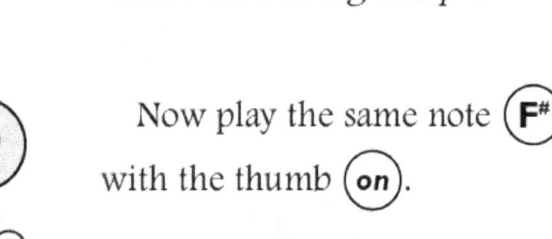

**39**

G to F#
trill

Now play the same note (**F#**) with the thumb (**on**).

This note is good for playing a **trill** beween **G** and **F#**. A trill is played by rapidly taking your second finger of the right hand on and off the key. You can do this quickly or slowly, but always evenly. We will be using trills for other notes.

Imprint the sound of (**F#**) high and **F#** low in your musical mind.

CH 3 – 5TH TUNE

# When I Fall In Love
## Heyman/Young (1957)

The famous ballad *When I Fall In Love* is where we are going to explore our sensual tone. The 1957 smash hit featuring the sublime voice of Nat King Cole inspired the heavyweight tenor saxualman, 'Big' Ben Webster, to record his own version. Ideally with headphones on, really wallow in this giant tone and fat 'vibrato' (coming soon) and bathe your burgeoning musical brain with this exotic sound.

The man Ben described as giving him his Ph.D in music, the legendary Duke Ellington, advised that to continually grow: "the most important thing is listening . . . that's the first step in becoming a musician. If and when they stop listening – to themselves or to somebody else, they're no longer with the music."

## CH 3 – 5TH TUNE

### *When I Fall In Love*

Verse 1  ¹When I fall in love / ²It will be for-ev-er /

**D    G C B G  /  D  G  C  B  G  A /**

³Or I'll nev-er fall in love /

**D  G  (E)(D)  C  B  A /**

⁴In a rest-less world like this is /

**B  C  (D)  G    G    G  B  A /**

⁵Love is end-ed be-fore it's be-gun /

**B   C (D) B  C (D) B  C (D) /**

⁶And too man-y moon-light kiss-es /

**C  (D)(E) A  A    A  C  B /**

⁷Seem to cool in the warmth of the sun /

**C   (D)(E) C (D)(E)   C (E)(D) /**

This song is in **G major** (happy). The only difference between **C major** and **G major** is that the **F** has been substituted by the **F#**. So the notes of **G major** are quite easy to play. Its relative minor is **E minor** (sad).

If you can learn verse 1, verse 2 is nearly the same so 'go for it'. Concentrate on tone. Play this as beautifully as

# When I Fall in Love

## When I Fall In Love

Verse 2  [8]When I give my heart / [9]It will be com-ple-tely /

**D    G C  B  G    /  D  G C B    G   A /**

[10]Or I'll nev-er give my heart /

**D G (E)(D) C  B  A   /**

[11]And the mo-ment I can feel that  /

**B   C (D) G  G G (F#)(E) /**

[12]You feel that way too /

**E  (E)(D)(E)  C  /**

[13]Is when I  fall in love . . . with you /

**A D   G C B G        A   G  /**

possible; play it to your loved one; play it with all the heart and soul you possess.

Now what we are going to do with *When I Fall in Love* is to make it more more like a personal song, because you are singing through your sax.

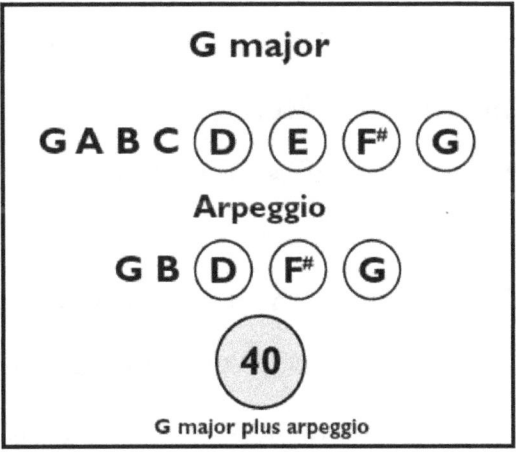

**G major**
G A B C (D) (E) (F#) (G)

**Arpeggio**
G B (D) (F#) (G)

(40)

G major plus arpeggio

## Ch 3 – Wah-Wahs

You can change the notes and make a song more musical and artistic by using staccato and legato and slurring (see Chapter 2). You can also bend one or more notes by using **Wah-Wahs** and **Woo-Woos** and **vibrato**.

We are going to be manipulating or changing the sound of a note. First, the **Wah-Wahs**.

What you do is a Steptoe & Son impersonation of the *'dirty old man'* and slide the bottom jaw up and down inside the mouth while keeping the lips steady, literally as though you are saying the Wah-Wah.

Try doing a Wah-Wah on (F#) – octave key (on). The jaw should drop and come back up, bending the note up and down from its natural pitch. Once you've done one Wah,

# Ch 3 – Wah-Wahs

keep the note steady at its natural pitch for a second or so before doing another Wah. Have a little break between them.

**41**
Wah-Wahs
(F#)

Drop the jaw — bring it back up — gap — evenly

If you drop the jaw too far, the note falls into the lower register, but you can drop it quite a long way before you lose the note. On the other hand, don't be afraid to let the jaw go. Your embouchure should be extremely relaxed and your bottom jaw should already be loose from active breathing.

Now do Wahs instead of tonguing when playing **G** (thumb **off**) in *When I Fall In Love*, phrases 4 and 11. Now it's coming alive and your own version will have some feel. You can make each Wah as long or as short as you think fits, but always leave a gap, otherwise the effect sounds like a lawnmower!

**42**
Wah-Wahs
G

Wahs generally sound more powerful with the thumb (**on**) in the upper register. It is a lazy, laidback bluesy sound.

## CH 3 – WOO-WOOS

**43**
Woo-Woos
(P)

The second type of note manipulation, called **Woo-Woos**, is more subtle. This is where you drop the jaw just a tiny bit. It sounds more like a *'blip'* in the note.

The Woo-Woos can be run together more closely than the Wah-Wahs, and can be played on any note. Keep it subtle, so it's there, but only just.

Wah-Wahs          Woo-Woos

Besides the Wahs and Woos, the other dominant force on your tone is **vibrato.** What is vibrato? Well, if you compare the *'singing'* of Johnny Rotten with that of Elvis Presley, you can hear the difference between a flat voice and the beautiful wavering on 'The King's' magnificent vocal delivery.

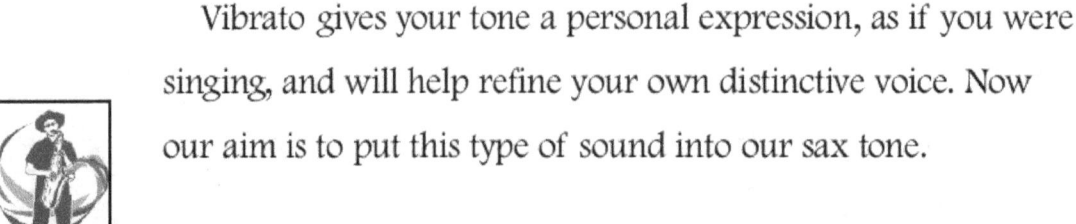

Vibrato gives your tone a personal expression, as if you were singing, and will help refine your own distinctive voice. Now our aim is to put this type of sound into our sax tone.

# CH 3 – VIBRATO

Vibrato is achieved by *mumbling* your lips, making the note slightly tremble. Think of when mama would *'whup'* you when you were in *Big Trouble* and you would be standing there with your bottom lip shaking uncontrollably.

The key is moving the lip and jaw ever so slightly to manipulate or change the sound of one long note. Be careful not to move too much as you might lose the quality of the tone. Try it on an easy note like the one we just learned, **F#**. Now try it with the octave key (on) ... (F#).

Try and make this mumble a very subtle waver, a ripple on the note, and not sounding too plain.

To make your vibrato even sweeter, try combining a little bit of the **Woo-Woo** with the slight mumble of the *bottom lip*. Incorporate this combination into your playing and make its presence felt, as without it the tone will often sound too plain.

# CH 3 – VIBRATO

If you can't feel this trembling sensation, play on a beach or in the garden at 3 a.m. and your chattering teeth will give you the heaviest wobble going on your tone – *'shiver into it!'*.

Vary the pulse so sometimes it is heavy and other times light. Experiment.

**45**
Varying the pulse slow to fast to slow

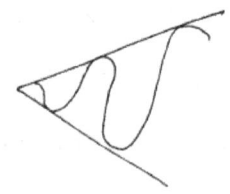

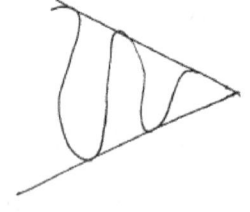

**46**
Foot tap

If you are still having problems try tapping a rhythm with your foot and playing the vibrato in time. Then try doubling it up while staying in time with the rhythm you are tapping.

Having a lovely vibrato floating through your tone is crucial to your **unique** sound. Imagine digestive biscuits with no choccy on top – *not very exciting*. That is what playing without vibrato sounds like. Compare this with a full

# Ch 3 – Vibrato

packet of chocolate digestives – *scoffed in minutes!* So, use vibrato sensitively, enough to flavour your tone but not to dominate it. Vibrato will become more natural the more you play it.

For a heavyweight vibrato, listen to Ben Webster or Dexter Gordon. This will give you the **idea** very, very clearly.

Now replay that master ballad by Nat King Cole, *When I Fall In Love*, and add Woos/lip vibrato, especially on the longer notes. And remember, love has many different meanings. Be in love with your sax like the first time you held it.

Concentrate on incorporating your Wahs and Woos into all of your tunes, so quite soon they will be there without you thinking about them.

# The First Time Ever I Saw Your Face
## Ewan MacColl (1963)

This sixth tune is one of the great songs of the 20th century. A youthful, romantic Archer first heard Roberta Flack sing it on her debut album of 1969, 'First Take' – and that version has retained its magic forever.

The record sleeve notes written by keyboard ace Les McCann say it all: "Roberta possesses, as a singer and a pianist, that rare quality which carries the listener beyond every barrier as though it never existed, to that level at which all humans can truly hear."

He goes on: "Roberta can take you all the way inside and clean your soul – out! And God said, 'That's good!' And I say, She sings her ass off!"

# The First Time . . .

Now as a saxophonist you have to continually find your own personal singing voice, one that can "sing a love song, and I was in love, we were all in love". So play this ballad as though you mean it – picture love and express it.

This song is in **E minor**, using the same notes as **G major** but starting on the **E**. Play it through, learn it, then personalise it by adding Wahs and Woos, vibrato and tonguing.

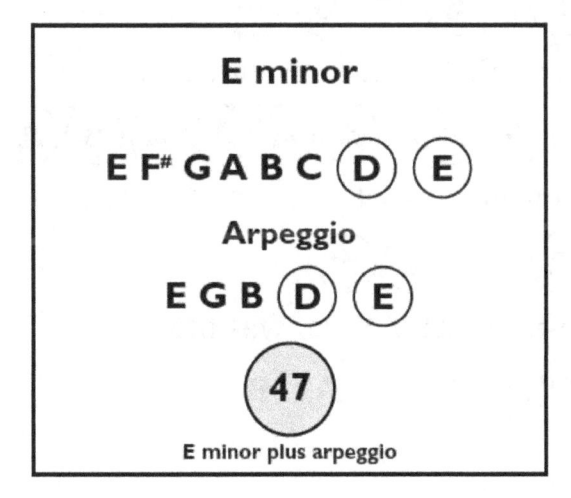

**E minor**

E F# G A B C (D) (E)

**Arpeggio**

E G B (D) (E)

(47)

E minor plus arpeggio

# 108     CH 3 – 6TH TUNE

## *The First Time Ever I Saw Your Face*

Verse 1   ¹The first time / ²Ev- er   I   saw your face /

(E) (E) (E) / (E) (F#) (G) (F#) (D) (A) /

³I thought the sun     /⁴rose in your eyes

(F#) (F#) (F#) (G) (F#) / (A) (A) (A) (A) (B) (A) (G) (F#) (G) /

⁵And the moon and the stars    / ⁶were the gifts you gave /

A   A   (A)   (A) (A) G (F#) / (F#) (E) (F#) (D) A /

⁷To the dark / ⁸and the end-less skies / ⁹my love /

A B C C / C C (D) (E) (D) / A A /

¹⁰To the dark / ¹¹and the end of the skies //

A B C C / A   A B   B A A //


Verse 2   ¹²The first time / ¹³Ev- er   I   kissed your mouth /

(E) (E) (E) / (E) (F#) (G) (F#) (D) (A) /

¹⁴I   felt the earth     /¹⁵move in my hands

(F#) (F#) (F#) (G) (F#) / (A) (A) (A) (A) (B) (A) (G) (F#) (G) /

¹⁶Like the trem-bling heart     /

(A) (A) (A) (A) G (F#) /

¹⁷Of   a   cap-tive bird / ¹⁸that was there /

(F#) (E) (F#) (D) A / A B C /

# The First Time . . .   *109*

## *The First Time Ever I Saw Your Face*

[19]At my command my love /

C D E D A A /

[20]That was there / [21]at my command / [22]my love //

A  B CCC / A B A A A / A A //

Verse 3  [23]And the first time / [24]ev- er  I  lay with you /

A  A E E / E F# G F# D A /

[25]I  felt your heart     / [26]so close to  mine           /

F# F# F# G F# / A A A A B A G F# G /

[27]And I knew our joy / [28]would fill  the earth /

A A A G F# / F# F# D A /

[29]And last / [30]til the end of time / [31]my love /

B  C / D D D D D / A A /

[32]And it would last / [33]til the end of time / [34]my love /

A  B C  C / A A B A A / A A /

Coda  [35]The first time / [36]Ev- er  I  saw           /

E  E  E / E F# G F# G F# E /

[37]your face / [38]your face / [39]your face     / [40]your face /

D  D / E  E / F# F# G / A A /

## CH 3 – C SHARP

**(48)** C#

The second of the sharps and flats is **C sharp** (written **C#**), also called **D flat** (**D♭**). Take all your fingers off all the keys but keep your fingers sitting *touch tight* over them. Keeping in mind that the **C#** takes the least amount of air, blow gently into the sax.

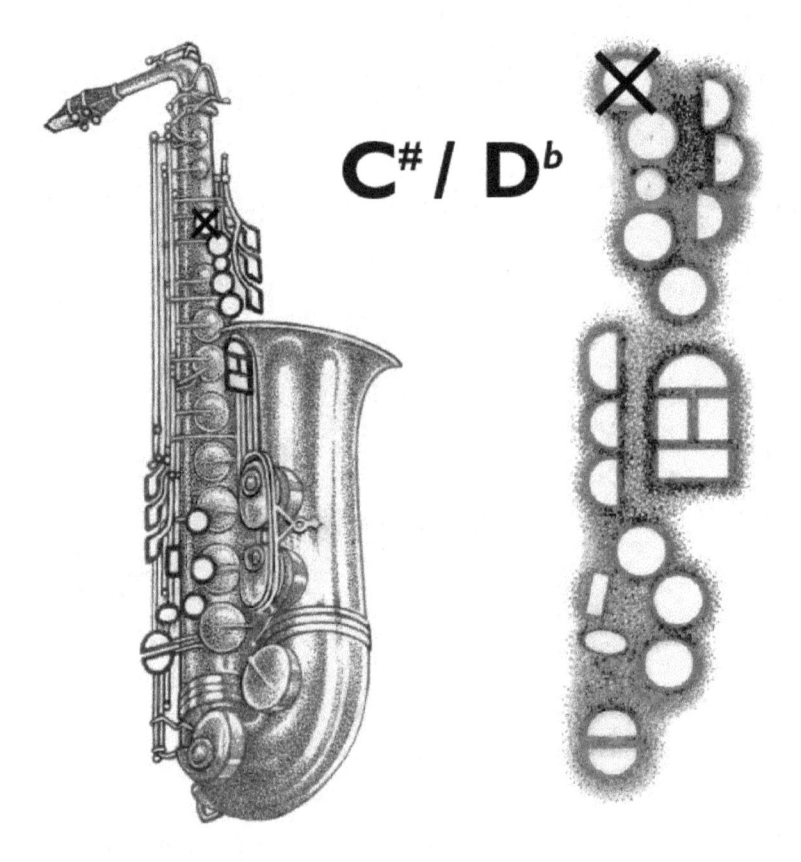

**C# / D♭**

*'The Ugliest Note'*

# Ch 3 – C Sharp

An easy one, but make sure the tone is even. It often sounds thin – think rich and full.

Now try playing it with the octave key (**on**). You have to slightly tighten the embouchure as this is now your new highest note. Think high and blow fast. You can check the top **C#** is in tune by simply taking the thumb **off** the octave key.

The way to remember the name of this note is to imagine Albert going to the optician to check that he can '*CCC sharp*'.

You will have noticed, I hope, that **C#** is the next note up from **C**. An explosive **trill**, though tricky to play, is between **C** and **C#**. This can be performed by using only the second finger of the left hand to play **C**, and flicking it on and off the key. Try this with thumb (**on**) and thumb **off**.

# Careless Whisper
## George Michael (1984)

The key ingredient to George Michael's massive white soul hit was Steve Gregory's alto sax pop miniature break. It's what we call a **hook**, straight into your forehead, never to be forgotten. It is one of those tunes that inspired and still inspires many to pick up the sax.

Spot the now obvious irony in this write-up: "Synths waft by on fluffy clouds, a Spanish guitar dedicatedly spells romance, and George bears his soul rather than his breast. The strangest thing is it works. There will not be a dry pair of knickers in the house." Colin Irwin, *Melody Maker*, 1984.

# Careless Whisper

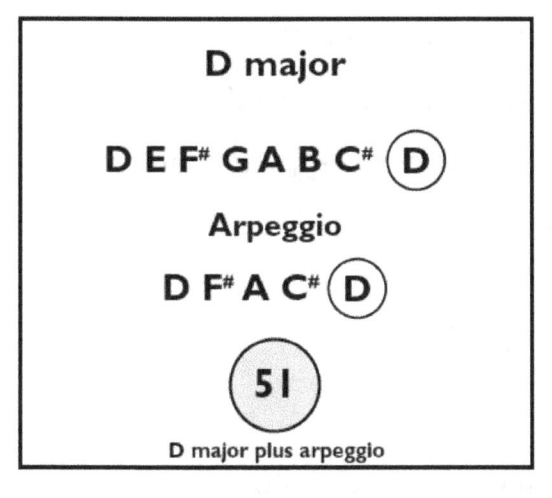

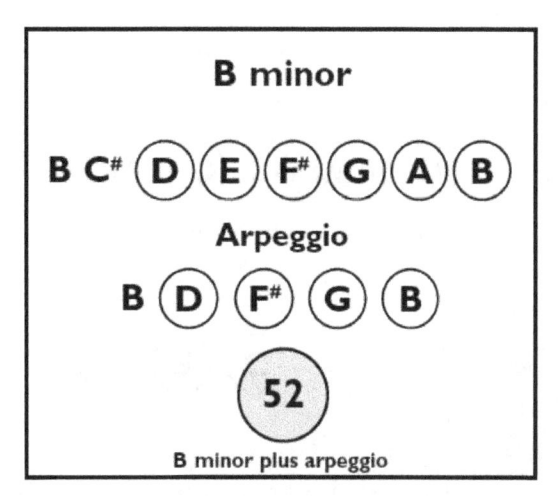

**D major**

D E F# G A B C# (D)

Arpeggio

D F# A C# (D)

(51)

D major plus arpeggio

**B minor**

B C# (D) (E) (F#) (G) (A) (B)

Arpeggio

B (D) (F#) (G) (B)

(52)

B minor plus arpeggio

The next set of scales is **D major**, whose relative minor is **B minor**. Work hard not to play **C** as it will be a bum note

To help you get into **D major** (happy) and **B minor** (sad) and used to playing **C#** you are going to play one of the greatest hooks of all time, which happens to be in **B minor**.

Now to start *Careless Whisper*, you have to learn to start with a **gliss**.

# Ch 3 – 7th Tune

**53**
Glisses
(D) to (C♯)

Glisses are a form of colour which are really dynamic. They are a *flick* of the fingers **away** from the keys, say (D) straight to (C♯) playing every note but very, very quickly. The way to do this is to play:

(D) (E) (F♯) (G) (A) (B) (C♯)

up and down *slowly but surely* and it will get faster, eventually flicking the whole movement up or down on as many notes as you like.

*Careless Whisper* and *Baker Street* are both examples of infamous hooks. Note on *Careless Whisper*, the gliss at the beginning will go from (D) to (C♯). Don't worry if you play any other notes because it is played so quickly, it's more of a blur.

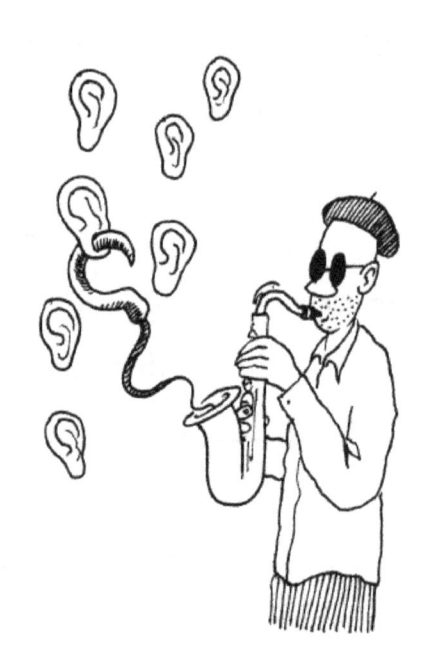

# Careless Whisper

*Careless Whisper*

1. (D) gliss↑ (C#) (B) (F#) (D) (C#) (B) (F#) (D) / (A) (G)

(D) B (A) (G) (D) /

2. (G) (F#) (D) B G /

3. F# G A B C# (D) (E) (F#) gliss↑ (C#) (B) (F#) (D) (C#)

(B) (F#) (D) /

4. (A) (G) (D) B (A) (G) (D) / 5. (G) (F#) (D) B G /

6. F# G A B C# (D) (E) (F#) //

---

## Chapter 3

### Sing through your Sax

We have learned:

- Two beautiful ballads and a famous sax hook
- Wahs, Woos and Vibrato
- Two new notes: **F#** and **C#**
- Glisses

"It's never hard to sing the blues.
Everyone in the world has the blues."
*John Lee Hooker*

## chapter four

# A Bluesy Interlude

We've introduced major scales and minor scales to you. There are others, of which the **blues** is a fabulous jamming scale. Play the **B blues** scale on the following pages up and down. Does it remind you of anything?

Very top notes coming in Chapter 7

**F** **F#** Trill key

There is an F to F# trill key. Use the third finger of the right hand to flick on and off the key

topF# topF topE topD B A F# F E D

blue note

blue note

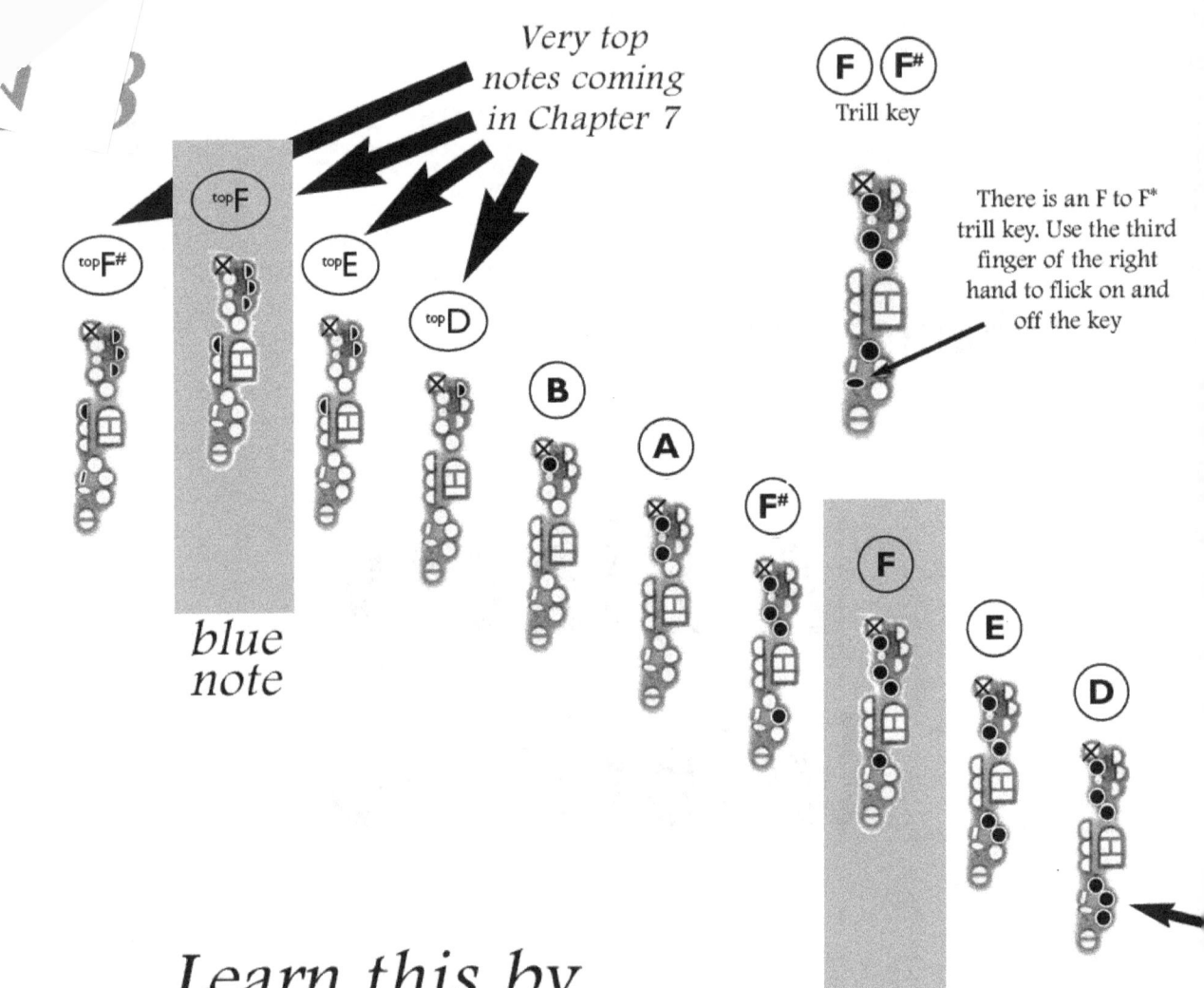

Learn this by heart.
Get it 'under your fingers'.

**Upper register**

# B Blues

## Play *only* these notes

## B D E F F# A B

blue note

*Start on B and play up scale*

*Very bottom notes coming in Chapter 6*

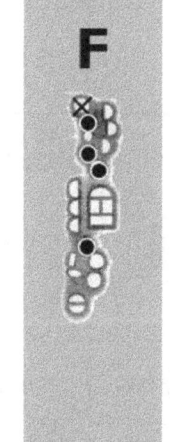

THE BRIDGE

**B**  **A**  **F#**  blue note **F**  **E**  **D**  bot **B**

Lower register

# CH 4 – B BLUES

I've given you the notes for the blues, so at any given point you just want to tap your foot and mess around with those notes. Even just running straight up and down the scale, you still sound pretty groovy, so that is the **B blues.**

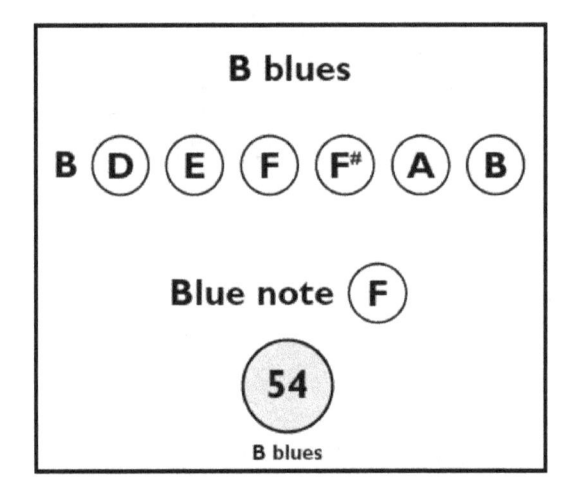

**B blues**

B (D) (E) (F) (F#) (A) (B)

Blue note (F)

(54)

B blues

# Ch 4 – 8th Tune

## St James Infirmary
### traditional

For a blues version of this much performed American folk song we go to New Orleans of the 1920s and a young Louis Armstrong, living on the edge while playing in the many clubs, surrounded by lowlife gamblers and pimps who ended up in the morgue. Louis's original approach to the depth and playfulness of the blues got him out of this treacherous world, but you can tell from the hint of melancholy in his vocal delivery and trumpet phrasing that he'd lived it. Even today, 'N'awlins' openly flaunts the spectre of death with crosses and funeral parlours throughout the town.

Listen to the CD and get the tune in your head. Wah-Wahs give a lovely soulful feel, the blues should be from the heart – so should your Wah-Wahs.

# 122     CH 4 – 8TH TUNE

## St James Infirmary

Verse 1   ¹ B (D) (F#) (F#) E (F#) (D) B /

**55** With sax

² B (D) (F#) (F#) (F#) B (G) (F#) /

³ B (D) (F#) (F#) E (F#) (D) B /

**56** Without sax

⁴ B (D) B (D) (D) B //

Verse 2   ⁵ (F#) (D) (F#) (F#) (F#) E (F#) (D) B F# /

⁶ B (D) (F#) (F#) / ⁷ (F#) (B) (G) (F#) /

⁸ (F#) (D) (F#) (F#) (F#) E (F#) (D) B /

⁹ (F) (D) B E (D) B B //

I went down to the St James infirmary
Saw my baby there
She was stretched out on a long white table
So sweet . . . so cold . . . so fair.

Let her go . . . let her go . . . god bless her
Wherever she may be
She can look this wide world over

But she'll never find a sweet man like me.

When I die want you to dress me in straight lace shoes
I wanna boxback coat and a stetson hat
Put a twenty dollar gold piece on my watch chain
So the boys'll know that I died standing flat.

# St James Infirmary

## *St James Infirmary*

Verse 3  10 (F#) (F#) (F#) / 11 (F#) (F#) (E) (F#) (D) B /

12 (F#) (F#) (B) (G) (F#) /

13 (F#) (F#) (F#) (F#) (F#) (E) (F#) (D) B /

14 (F) (F) (E) (D) (D) B A B /

Verse 4  15 (B) (B) (B) (B) (B) (B) (B) (B) (B) /

16 (F#) (B) (B) (B) (G) (F#) /

17 (F#) (F#) (F#) (F#) (F#) (E) (F#) (D) B /

18 B (D) (F) (F) (F) (F) (E) (D) B /

19 B (D) (F) (F) (F) (F) (E) (D) B /

20 B (D) (F) (F) (F) (E) (D) B /

Concentrate on keeping in time with the music. Get the tune running in your head, hum it, sing it, get it really firmly ensconced in your bonce. Play it on your own and then try and play it with the music.

# CH 4 – 9TH TUNE

# Mourning Blues
## Archer

The ninth tune is a little track we've written called *Mourning Blues*. You are still in B blues, it's a lovely solo track, and you don't need any accompaniment.

# Mourning Blues

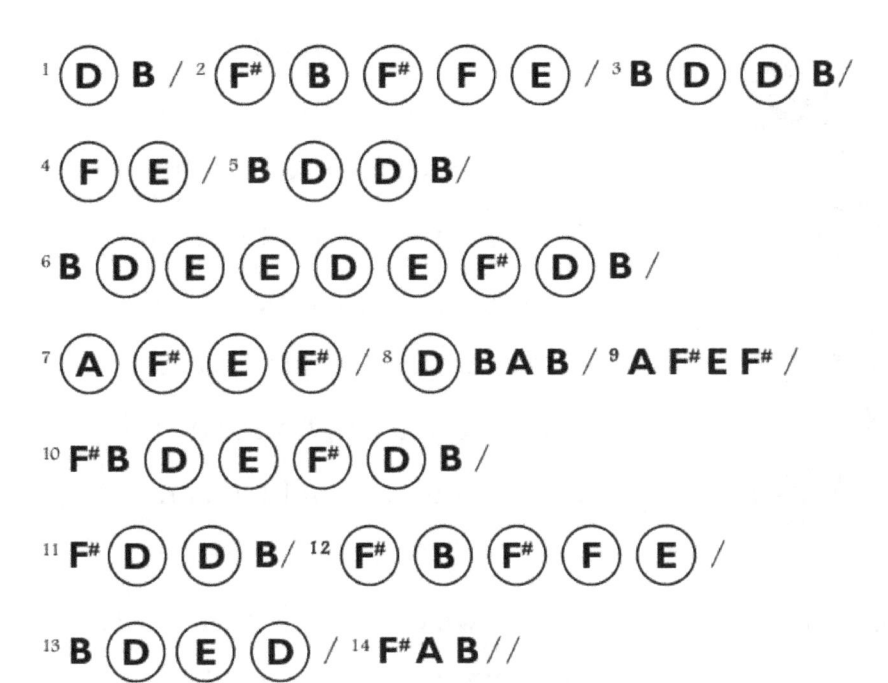

**125**

57

¹ D B / ² F# B F# F E / ³ B D D B/
⁴ F E / ⁵ B D D B/
⁶ B D E E D E F# D B /
⁷ A F# E F# / ⁸ D B A B / ⁹ A F# E F# /
¹⁰ F# B D E F# D B /
¹¹ F# D D B/ ¹² F# B F# F E /
¹³ B D E D / ¹⁴ F# A B //

One of my great desires when learning the sax was to play something that was soulful. Now sax can be happy – equally it can be sad. So we are going to do a little bit of blues. We will play this tune to you, then show you an amazing growling effect.

So, *Mourning Blues*, slowly . . . just a lovely miserable blues track, but "we like a bit of that".

## CH 4 – GROWLING

Now it is time for you to learn how to Growl. This can be your pet project to do when totally *'blitzed'*, knee-buckled, blasted because you need to be *'out-to-lunch'* to perform this sound, otherwise you can think about it too hard and it won't happen.

**58**
Funky Growl

The first way is a **Funky** Growl, officially called *Flutter Tonguing*. Simply roll your *RRRRRRRRs* while blowing out hard. Try this first without the sax in your mouth. You'll look like a horse snorting. That's the trick, **before** trying to make a Growl on the sax. Some folks can do this and some cannot.

The way to do it with the sax is to start rolling the *RRRRRs* really hard in the roof of the mouth and then slowly glide the mouthpiece into the mouth **not tightening** the mouth at all and then the *'dirtying'* and *'rumbling'* of the sound will happen. Try this on an **B**.

## CH 4 – GROWLING – BUZZ

Once this is working, control the power of the *RRRRRs* so you can vary how subtle or rugged you want it to come across.

The second way is more a **Buzz**. The way to do it is to buy a *kazoo*, act like an irritating child, and blow it making the noise at the top of your throat. Remember this sensation, then grab the sax and try to duplicate it.

Other ways to do this are to sing like Louis Armstrong with his gravelly voice, or by gargling water. The easiest way is simply to *hum*. If you can *hum* the note you are playing, it sounds even sweeter.

## CH 4 – GROWLING – KICKER

This is the only time I'll say blow as hard as you can and push from your guts, as normally you'll blow more softly. Remember, you are trying to bump the air into the mouthpiece. Try mixing these two together.

**60**
Kicker

The third way I call a **Kicker**. For this you have to have some *phlegm* in the back of your throat as though you are about to spit. This is a harsh and **vicious** sound. It only has one problem; that the head is so full of the noise from the throat that you can't hear its effect on the note and of course sustaining the phlegm is difficult. However this is a **wicked** Growl.

The key to a successful Growl is to roll your *RRRRS*, hum, gargle and spit, while blowing out as hard as you can, before trying it out on the sax. Try all the types and use them all.

# CH 4 – Summary

> **Chapter 4**
> *A Bluesy Interlude*
> **Summary**
> We have learned:
> • Our first super cool Blues scale
> • Two Blues tunes
> • Raunchy, raw Growls

The Growl changes the tone **radically** and makes it **raunchy** and **raw.** Most importantly it gives the sax a real *human voice* and scream.

"A genius! For thirty-seven years I've practised fourteen hours a day and now they call me a genius."
*Pablo Sarasate*

chapter five

# Two Little Fingers & B Flat

In this chapter we are going to show you the last three basic notes:

**G sharp (G#)**

**D sharp (D#)**

**B flat (B♭)**

# CH 5 – G SHARP

**CD2**

( 1 )
G#

The next note gives your little finger a reason for existence, no longer just to wear pretty rings. If you look at your horn, you will see that the **G** key has been designed by Father Sax, to stick out a little bit. Now to play **G#**, hold the three left-hand fingers down and pull the left-hand little finger out of retirement, placing it on the shift key it has been sitting over. Watch out because the **G#** pad sometimes sticks.

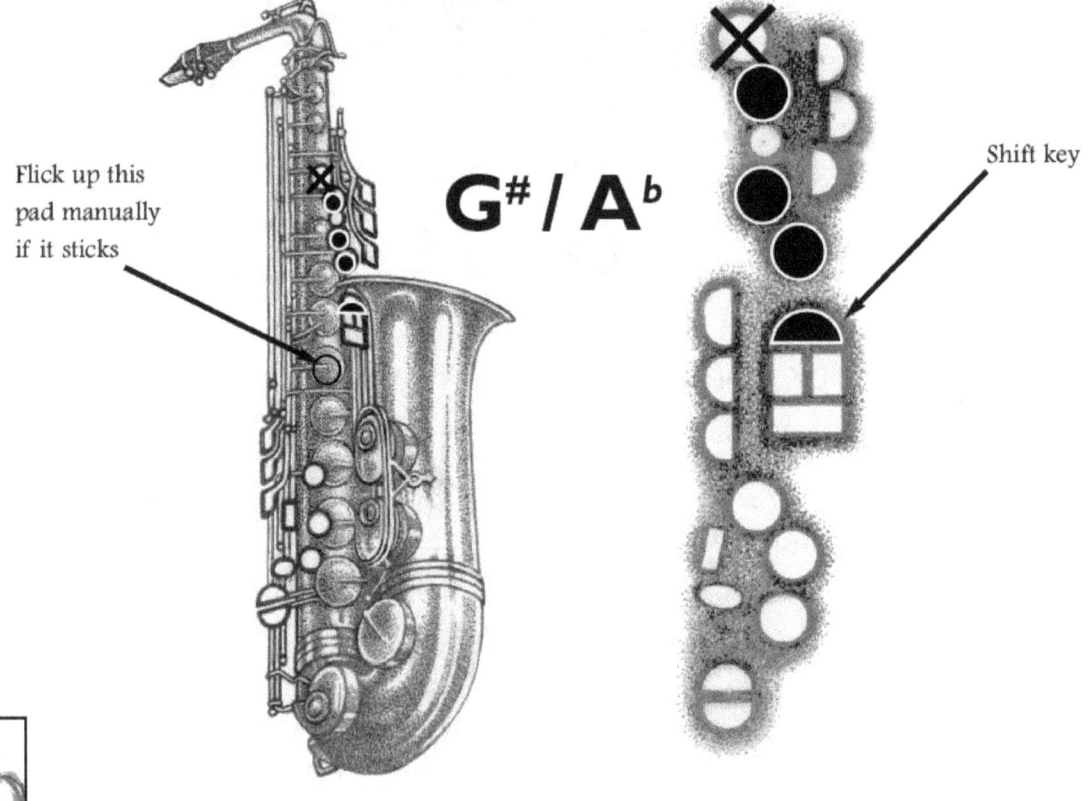

**G# / A♭**

Flick up this pad manually if it sticks

Shift key

# Ch 5 – G Sharp

Now's your chance to train your *'pinky'*. Taking care to hold down **G**, flick the little finger on and off, trilling from **G** to **G#**, building up strength and control.

Memorise this note by imagining Uncle Sam taking a bite out of a lemon and saying, *'Gee, sharp'*.

Now put the thumb **(on)** the octave key and blow the higher note **(G#)**/**(A♭)** cleanly. Again, if it sounds at all *'grumbly'* you are swallowing a little too much mouthpiece. Move your mouth a tiny bit towards the tip. The note should now sound pure.

So, we now know the notes **F#**, **C#** and **G#**. Make sure you can play these comfortably before you move on. That's the order so far! Three down, two to go.

## CH 5 – 10TH TUNE

# Brahms' Lullaby

In John O'Farrell's hilarious and confessional *The Best a Man Can Get*, the main character describes this tune thus: "I put the kids back to bed and wound up the mobile which produced a tinny version of *Brahms' Lullaby*, the official theme song of every nursery in the land, chosen for its universal popularity, its gentle melody, but mainly for the fact that its copyright expired two centuries ago."

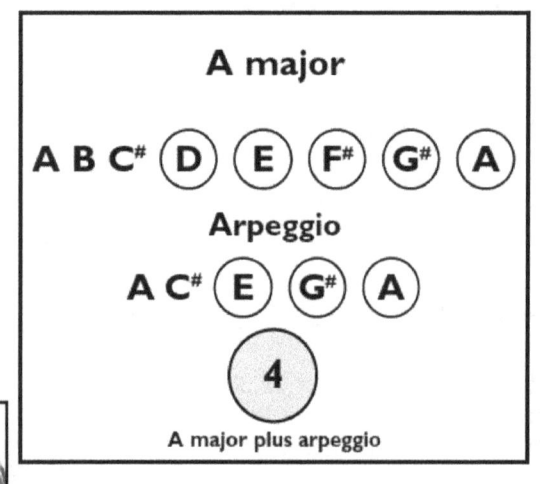

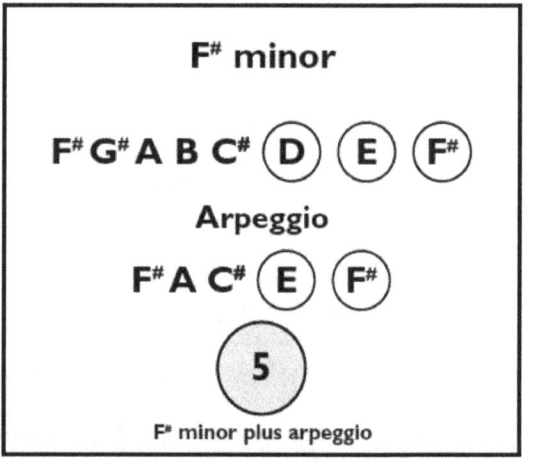

**A major**

A B C# (D) (E) (F#) (G#) (A)

Arpeggio

A C# (E) (G#) (A)

(4)

A major plus arpeggio

**F# minor**

F# G# A B C# (D) (E) (F#)

Arpeggio

F# A C# (E) (F#)

(5)

F# minor plus arpeggio

# Brahms' Lullaby

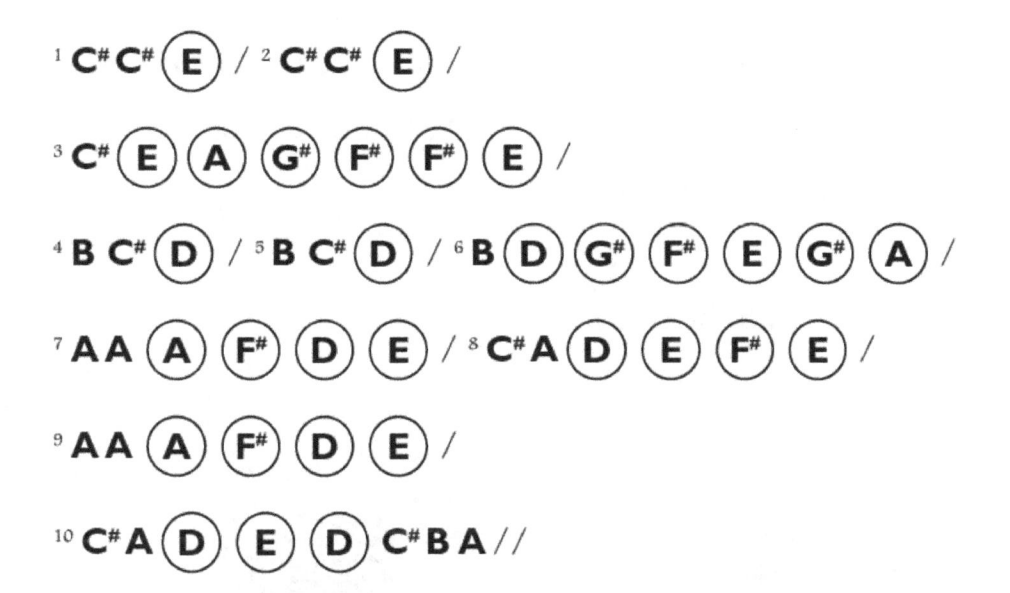

### 135

¹ C♯ C♯ (E) / ² C♯ C♯ (E) /

³ C♯ (E) (A) (G♯) (F♯) (F♯) (E) /

⁴ B C♯ (D) / ⁵ B C♯ (D) / ⁶ B (D) (G♯) (F♯) (E) (G♯) (A) /

⁷ A A (A) (F♯) (D) (E) / ⁸ C♯ A (D) (E) (F♯) (E) /

⁹ A A (A) (F♯) (D) (E) /

¹⁰ C♯ A (D) (E) (D) C♯ B A //

**6** With sax

**7** Without sax

As you start phrase 6, while crossing the bridge from **B** to (D), place your left hand little finger down on the (G♯) key and leave it there until you play the last but one note of that phrase. It makes playing (G♯) so much easier.

I once saw Dave Brubeck conclude a gig by preceding the last number with this lullaby. It worked then, as it will now – and it will get your 'pinkies' playing those sharps.

The song is in **A major / F♯ minor**.

# Ch 5 – D Sharp

**8**
D#/E♭

**9**
D#/E♭
on

On to **D#** (**E♭**). Put all six fingers on for normal **bottom D**, and add the right-hand little finger, nudging the upper part of the two-part key.

Now try with the octave key (**on**).

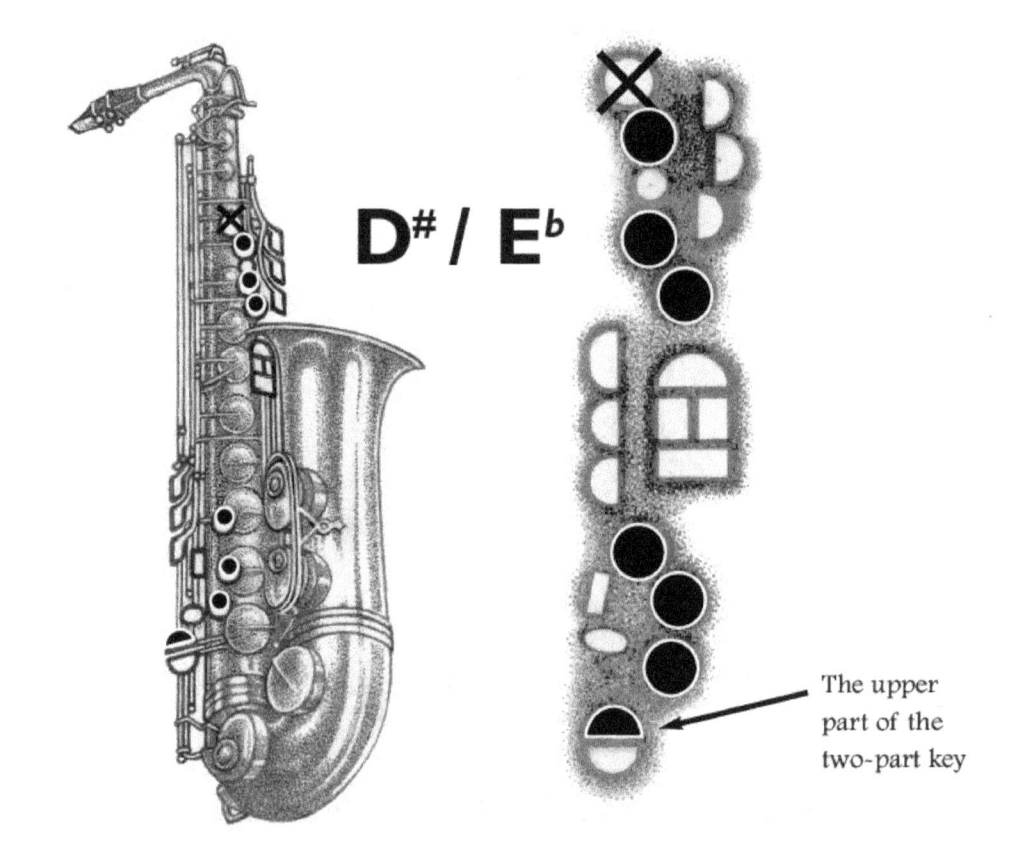

# D# / E♭

The upper part of the two-part key

# CH 5 – D SHARP

### 137

Remember when playing the lower **D♯/E♭** - thumb **off** - to blow softly, with a relaxed bottom lip and push from the stomach. This will ensure the note is rich and deep.

Introducing that legendary soul diva, *Dee Sharpe*.

Now put the thumb **(on) (D♯)** and trill with the right-hand little finger. Keep trilling with the little *'pinky'* until it develops its own pectoral muscles.

**10**

D♯/E♭ to D
(on)
trill

# 138    CH 5 – 11TH TUNE

# John Brown's Body
## (1861)

**11** *With sax*

**12** *Without sax*

This old Republican marching song of the American Civil War works big time for any voice, slow or fast. The version on the CD is slow so you can work on your technique to get it absolutely perfect. The tune is in **E major / C# minor**. For you Manchester United fans, it's what they sing at 'the theatre of dreams'.

Verses 1 and 2

¹John Brown's bo-dy lies  a  mould-ring in the grave /
**B   B     G# B (E) (F#) (G#) (G#) (G#) (F#) (E) /**

²John Brown's bo-dy lies  a mould-ring in the grave /
**C#  C#   (E)(D#)(E) C# B  C#   B A G#  /**

³John Brown's bo-dy lies  a  mould-ring in the grave /
**B   B     G# B (E) (F#) (G#) (G#) (G#) (F#) (E) /**

⁴But his soul goes march-ing on /
**(E)(E)(F#)(F#) (E) (D#)(E) /**

# John Brown's Body

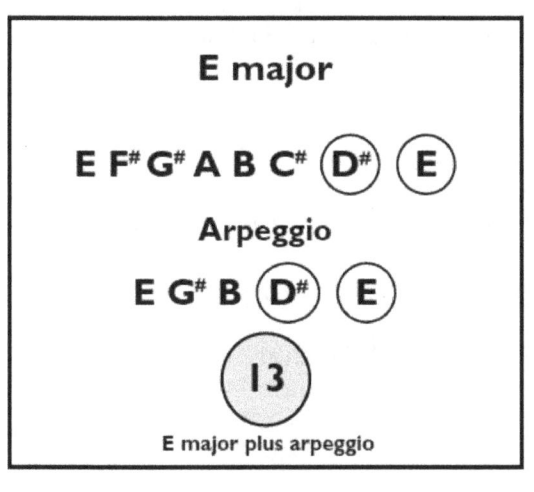

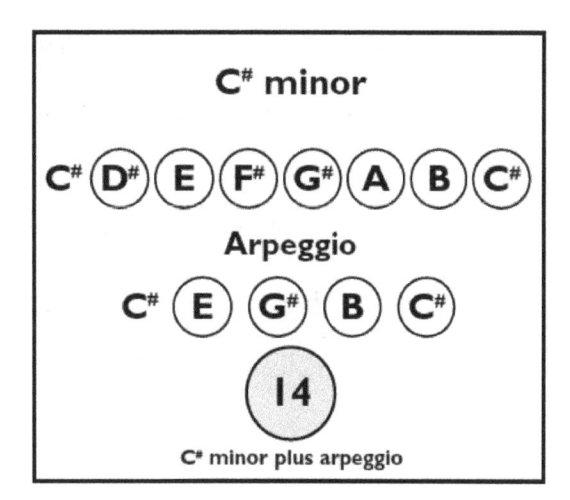

### E major
E F# G# A B C# (D#) (E)

**Arpeggio**
E G# B (D#) (E)

(13)

E major plus arpeggio

### C# minor
(C#)(D#)(E)(F#)(G#)(A)(B)(C#)

**Arpeggio**
(C#)(E)(G#)(B)(C#)

(14)

C# minor plus arpeggio

Chorus ⁵Glo-ry, Glo-ry Hal- le- lu- jah /
B A G# B (E)(F#)(G#)(E) /
⁶Glo-ry, Glo-ry Hal- le- lu- jah /
(C#)(D#)(E)(D#)(E) C# B A G# /
⁷Glo-ry, Glo-ry Hal- le- lu- jah /
B A G# B (E)(F#)(G#)(F#)(E) /
⁸And his soul goes march-ing on /
(E)(E)(F#)(F#)(E)(D#)(E) //

# Ch 5 – B Flat

**(15) B♭**

That's the four sharps. Now for the final note, **B flat (B♭)**, also known as **A sharp (A♯)**.

Use the first finger of the left hand to cover the **B** and the diddy key below it called the **'bis' key**. Make sure you only use your index finger to cover both keys. Blow that sweet note.

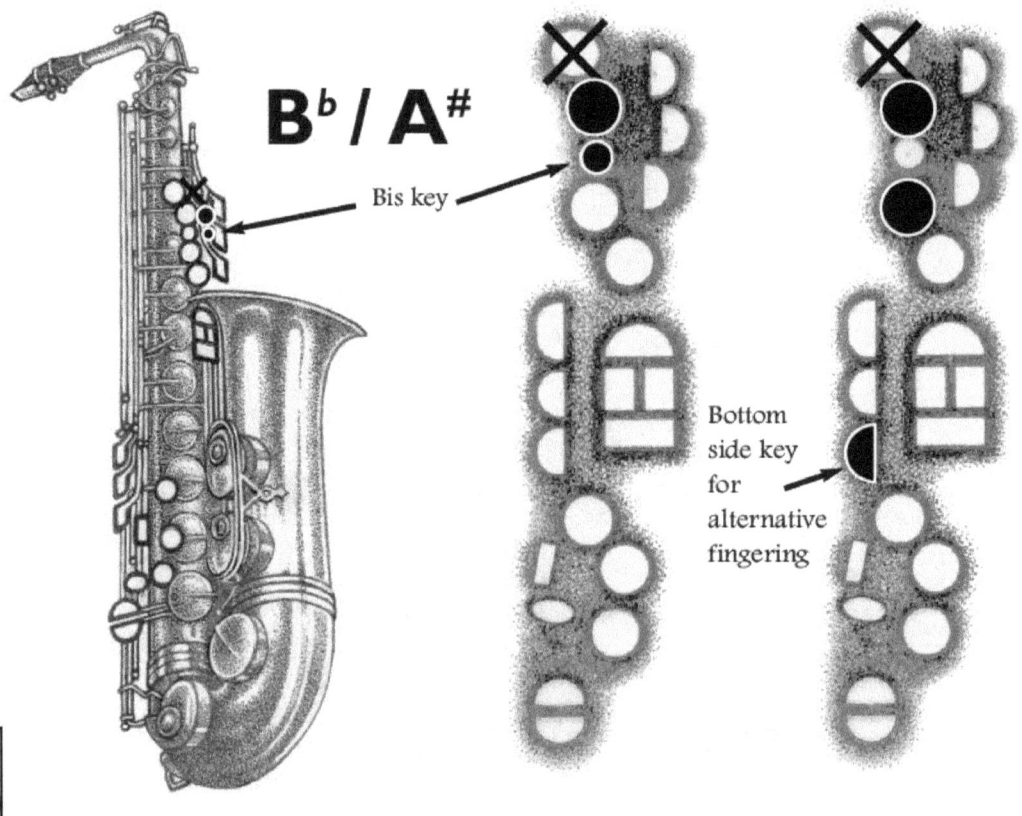

**B♭ / A♯**

Bis key

Bottom side key for alternative fingering

## CH 5 – B FLAT

*Or* finger the **A** and add the bottom **side key**. Use them both. More often than not we will be using our bis **B**$^b$.

Use the side **B**$^b$ when approaching it from **A** or **B**.

So when you're playing this,

*Be Flat.*

Now put the thumb **(on)** and play the higher **(B**$^b$**)**. Think high. Check the top is in tune simply by taking the thumb **off** the octave key. Again, slightly tighten the top lip if the note needs it.

# 142

## CH 5 – 12TH TUNE

# House of the Rising Sun
### traditional folk song

**17** *With sax*

**18** *clean*

Let's end this chapter with a classic. Arranged by Alan Price and produced by the late Mickie Most, the Animals' version of this traditional folk song first recorded by Nina Simone became an instant US/UK number one in 1964.

**G blues**

G B♭ C C♯ (D) (F) (G)

**Blue note C♯**

**19**
G blues

# HOUSE OF THE RISING SUN   143

Verse 1  There is / a house / in New Or-leans /

    G  G / A B♭ / (D) C  G  G  /

They call the Ris-ing Sun /

(G) (G) (G) (F) (D) (D) /

And it's be-en the ruin / of many a poor boy /

(G) (G) (G) / G A B♭ / (D) C  G  F  G /

And God, / I know / I'm one /

G  G  / G F# D / F# G /

Verse 2  My mother was a tail-or / She sewed my new blue jeans /

(G)(G)(G)(G)(F)(D) C G / (G)(G)(G)(F)(D)(D) /

My father was a gam-blin' man / Down in New Or-leans /

(G)(G)(G)(F)(D) C  G  B♭ / G  G F# D  F# G /

Verse 3  Now the on-ly thing a gam-bler needs /

(G)(G)(G)(G)(F)(D) C  G  B♭ /

Is a suit-case and a trunk /

(G)(G)(G)(G)(F)(D)(D) /

And the on-ly time he's sat-is-fied /

(G)(G)(G)(G)(F)(D) C  G  B♭ /

Is when he's on a drunk /

G G  F#  D F# G  /

# 144 CH 5 – 12TH TUNE

## *House of the Rising Sun*

Verse 4  Well I got one foot on the plat-form /
Ⓖ Ⓖ Ⓖ Ⓖ Ⓕ Ⓓ C  G       /
The oth-er on the train /
Ⓖ Ⓖ Ⓖ Ⓕ Ⓓ Ⓓ /
I'm goin' back to New Or-leans /
Ⓖ Ⓖ Ⓖ Ⓕ Ⓓ C  G  B♭ /
To wear that ball and chain /
**G  G  G  F♯ D  F♯  G** /

Verse 5  Well there is a house in New Or-leans /
Ⓖ Ⓖ Ⓖ Ⓖ Ⓕ Ⓓ C  G  B♭ /
They call the Ris-ing Sun /
Ⓖ Ⓖ Ⓕ Ⓓ Ⓓ /
And it's been the ruin of many a poor boy /
Ⓖ Ⓖ Ⓖ Ⓕ Ⓓ C  G   G /
And God, I know I'm one /
**G  G  G  F♯  F♯  G** /

# CH 5 – FOUR SHARPS & B FLAT 145

Know how to play all of your new notes. Really *listen* to each note and try from the start to remember what each one actually sounds like.

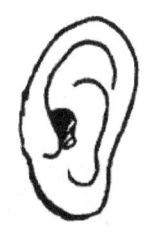

Use the cartoons to remember the names of these four sharps and B flat. When you go to blow any of these notes, make sure you can play them easily.

When you put these five notes together with the seven naturals, you've got your 12 crucial notes. This totals 24 notes, higher and lower register, and you'll play these most of the time.

This is your **foundation** so build it securely and above all *enjoy* playing.

# 146    Ch 5 – Four Sharps & B Flat

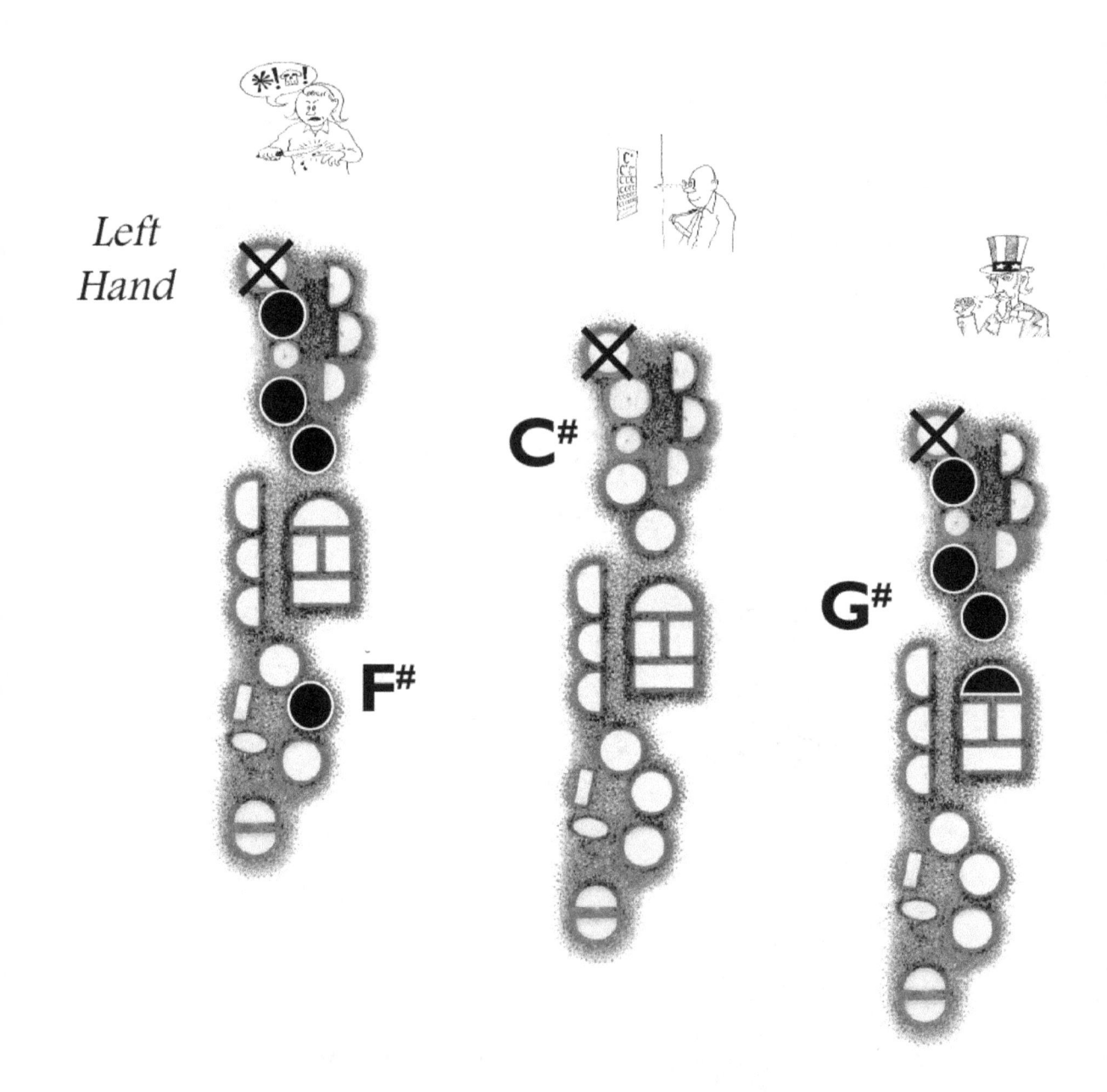

**Left Hand**

F#

C#

G#

Remember the order these notes come in.
*Fab Crazy Gang Down Beach.*
You'll use this order again and again!

# Ch 5 – Four Sharps & B Flat    *147*

## *4 Sharps & B Flat*

24/33

Octave Key **on** or **off**

**D#**

**B♭**

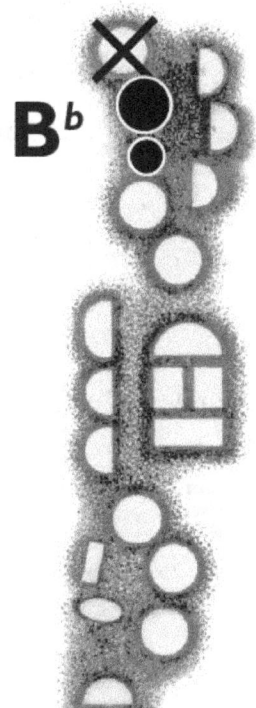

*Right Hand*

# 148    CH 5 – BEFRIEND THE KEYS

If you want your fingers to **befriend** the four sharps and B flat quickly, use the *non-blowing* method mentioned on pages 60 and 61. This helps your finger co-ordination tremendously.

The order to remember forever is:

## F# C# G# D# + B♭

The way to remember this is **F**ab **C**razy **G**ang **D**own **B**each.

# CH 5 – TWO LITTLE

*149*

### Chapter 5
### *Two Little Fingers and B Flat*
#### Summary
We have learned:
- Three new notes: **G♯**, **D♯** and **B♭**
- Three massively famous tunes

*150*

"The pain passes but the beauty remains." Auguste Renoir

## chapter six

# Very Bottom Notes

We are well on our way to completing the final eight notes that we need to know to give us all 32 notes on the sax. There are four keys for the very *top* notes, and four notes at the **very bottom**.

**No more mystery.**

# Ch 6 – Bottom C

Now that your breathing and embouchure have developed and your fingers are working sweetly we are ready to go for these glorious notes. If you find the following notes incredibly difficult when the other 24 notes are playing easily, try another reed. If you are then still having problems, your horn might not be working properly. Get it checked out.

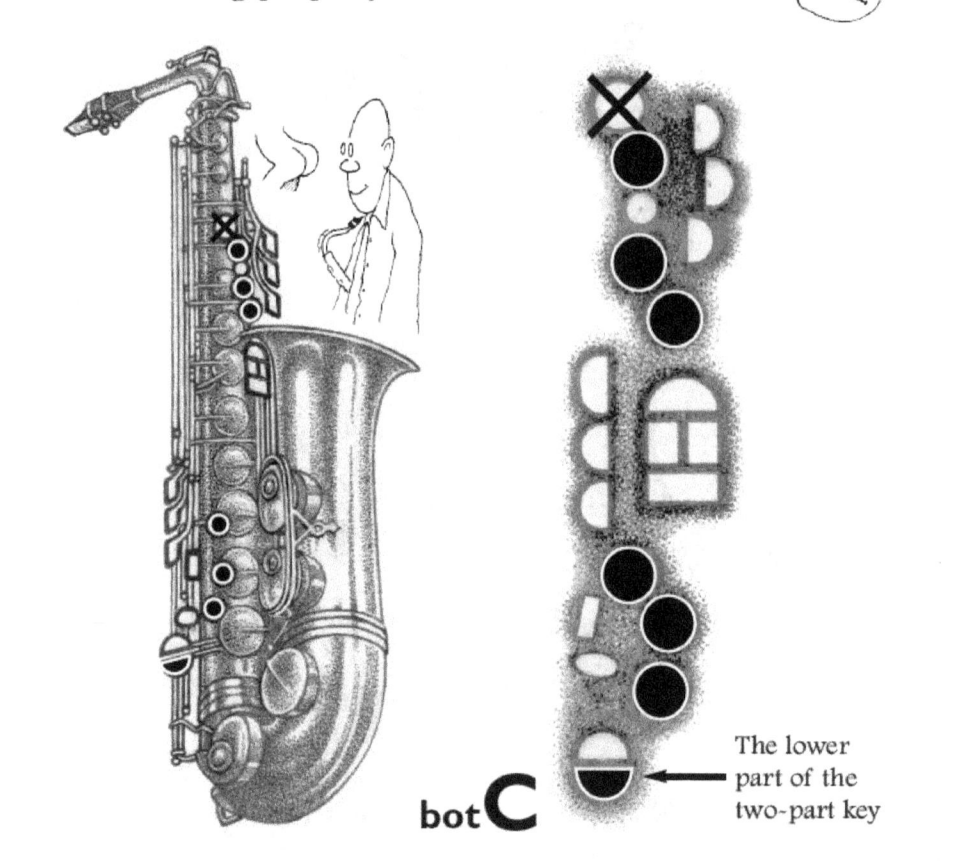

**20** botC

bot **C**

The lower part of the two-part key

# CH 6 – BOTTOM C

The very bottom notes. Now with the octave key **off**, play bot**C**, which we first tried on page 48 – put six fingers down and add the right-hand little finger on the lower part of the two-part key. Push from the **tum** and blow slowly and gently. Remember to *relax the bottom lip* and **think low**.

The **secret** to achieving all the bottom notes is to blow as if you are *running out of air*. Just put in enough puff to make the note sound, otherwise you'll get the foghorn effect. Try to slow the air flow that you put into the sax, and slightly relax the pressure off the bottom part of the reed. It makes the mouth and the head *vibrate* like crazy!

Always play it as bot**C** – *never* use this fingering with the octave key (**on**). Otherwise the note has a split personality. Sometimes it comes out as **C** sometimes as (**G**).

## 154   CH 6 – 1st Tune Revisited

### *Camptown Races* (high)

Verse 1  Camp-town la- dies sing that song / ²Doo-dah  Doo-dah/

Ⓖ   ⒼⒺⒼⒶⒼⒺ/  ⒺⒹⒺⒹ/

³Camp-town race track five miles long/

Ⓖ   Ⓖ Ⓔ Ⓖ Ⓐ Ⓖ Ⓔ /

⁴Oh! De-doo-dah day! /

Ⓓ ⒻⒺⒹ C /

Chorus  ⁵Gwine to run  all night! /  ⁶Gwine to  run all  day! /

C   CⒺⒼC  /  Ⓐ  ⒶCⒶⒼ /

⁷I'll bet  my mon-ey on de bob-tail nag /

ⒼⒼⒺ   Ⓖ  ⒶⒼⒺ/

⁸Some-bod- y  bet  on de bay.

Ⓓ     ⒻⒺⒹ  C

We are going to bring back *Camptown Races* as your fingers already know this one. We are going to drop it an octave and play it **really low**. Check it out.

# Camptown Revisited
### 155

## *Camptown Races* (low)

Verse 2  ⁹I came down dah wid my hat caved in/ ¹⁰Doo-dah Doo-dah/
        **G   G   E   G       A   G   E /   E   D   E   D /**

¹¹I go back home wid a pocket full of tin /
    **G   G   E   G   A   G       E /**

¹²Oh!         Doo-dah day! /
    **D     F   E   D   botC /**

Chorus ¹³Gwine to run all night! / ¹⁴Gwine to run all day! /
    **botC   botC   E   G   C /   A       A   C   A   G /**

¹⁵I'll bet my mon-ey on de bob-tail nag /
    **G   G   E   G   A   G   E /**

¹⁶Some-bod-y bet on de bay./
    **D     F   E   D   botC /**

**21** High and Low versions with sax

**22** High and Low versions without sax

Play along with that exquisite gentle rendition and then with that *Blazin' Saddles*-style lowdown, cowboy saloon bar version – over in a full and speedy 38 seconds.

# Pop Goes the Weasel
## traditional

This ditty has always been 'under my fingers' since seeing the top movie *A Rage in Harlem*, where the principal villain utters the fatal order with *Pop Goes the Weasel*.

There are no great difficulties with the tune other than the point where you've got to bang off the **botC** (phrases 2 and 3). Now with bottom notes you can either play them softly or, in this case, you can 'bang' it quite hard. Just push with your stomach.

The other bit to remember is when you play **C♯** to the **(D)** (phrases 4 and 8), you are going from no fingers with the octave key **off** to all six fingers with the octave key **(on)**. This is called a **grace note**. Remember to keep these fingers *touch tight* to the keys. So, let your fingers literally dance while playing *Pop Goes the Weasel*.

# Pop Goes the Weasel

### 157

1-8 x 3  ¹All a-round the cob-bler's bench /

   **F  F  G   G  A  C   A  F /**

²The mon-key chased the wea-sel /

bot**C  F   F   G   G  A  F /**

³The mon-key thought 'twas all in fun /

bot**C  F  F  G   G    A  C  A  F /**

⁴Pop!    Goes the wea-sel /

**C#** (**D**) **G  B♭ A  F /**

⁵A half a pound of two-pen-ny rice /

**C**(**F**)(**E**)(**D**)(**F**)(**E**)(**G**)(**E**) **C /**

⁶A half a pound of trea-cle /

**C**(**F**)(**E**)(**D**)(**F**)(**E**) **C/**

⁷That's the way the mon-ey goes

  **B♭  A  B♭  C** (**D**)(**E**)(**F**)

⁸Pop!    Goes the wea-sel /

**C#** (**D**) **G  B♭ A  F /**

⁹Pop!    Goes the wea-sel / ¹⁰Pop!    Goes the wea-sel /

**C#** (**D**) **G  B♭ A  F / C#** (**D**) **G  B♭ A  F /**

23

## What a Wonderful World
### Bob Thiele/George David Weiss (1967)

A classic UK No.1 that almost didn't happen. Bob Thiele, who co-wrote the tune under the pseudonym George Douglas, was recording it with Louis Armstrong when his boss, ABC Records' president, barged in and blew his top. He had just had a major hit with *Hello, Dolly* and now he was doing a ballad? The ABC president ordered everyone out.

Thiele screamed in protest, and the president finally left, but he refused to promote the record. It hit UK No. 1 in 1968, but had to wait many years before becoming a US hit on the back of Robin Williams's brilliant performance in the film *Good Morning Vietnam* in 1988.

# WHAT A WONDERFUL WORLD  *159*

Satchmo's unique voice was once described by Earl Hines thus: "Every cat in Chicago will stick his head out of the window when it rains so that they can sound like Louis".

Louis 'Pops' Armstrong used to set up his own 'wonderful world' by starting every day with his twin addictions to herbal laxatives and herbal relaxitives. After these indulgences, he would say, he'd "leave it all behind".

The very first phrase starts with a **bot****C**. Blow softly when you start this note and tease it out. The note also appears at phrase 13 after four consecutive **G**s, so have your right hand poised *touch tight* to the keys and **think low**.

When you go from **bot****C** to **B**$^b$ a good tip is to have the first finger over the **B**$^b$ (bis key) – see page 140 – when you are holding the right hand keys down. Then you are prepared to play the **B**$^b$.

# 160    CH 6 – 14TH TUNE

## *What a Wonderful World*

Verses 1 and 2

¹/⁷I see trees of green / ²/⁸Red ros- es too /

botC   E   F   F   C   /   Ⓓ Ⓓ Ⓓ C /

³/⁹I see them bloom / ⁴/¹⁰For me and you /

B♭ B♭ B♭   A   /   G G G F /

⁵/¹¹And I think to my-self /

F   F   F   F F F /

⁶/¹²What a won-der-ful world /

⁶   F   F E F G A /

¹² F   F E F G F /

Bridge   ¹³The col-ours of the rain-bow/ ¹⁴So pre-tty in the sky /

F   G   G   G   G   botC / botC B♭ A A G♯ A /

¹⁵Are al-so on the fa-ces / ¹⁶Of peo-ple go-ing by /

F   G   G G G G / botC B♭ A A A A /

¹⁷I see friends shak-in' hands / ¹⁶Say-in' "How do you do?" /

A C Ⓓ   Ⓓ Ⓓ C   /   A   A Ⓓ Ⓓ Ⓓ C /

¹⁹They're rea-lly say-ing "I love you" /

Ⓓ   Ⓓ Ⓓ C C B♭ A G /

# What a Wonderful World

## *What a Wonderful World*

Verse 3   ²⁰I hear ba-bies cry-in' / ²¹I watch them grow /

**bot C E F F C**    /   (**D**)(**D**)   (**D**) **C**   /

²²They'll learn much more / ²³Than I'll ever know /

**B♭   B♭   B♭   A**   /   **G   G G   F**   /

²⁴And I think to my-self /

**F F F   F F F**   /

²⁵What a won-der-ful world /

**F   F E F G A**   /

²⁶Yes, I think to my-self /

**A F A   F G G F**   /

²⁷What a won-der-ful world /

**F   F E F G F**   /

²⁸Oh Yeah! /

**F A**   /

To personalise things, try mixing different types of articulation: **legato**, **vibrato**, **wahs** and **woos** (see Chapter 3).

# 162

## Ch 6 – Bottom C Sharp

Listen to the recordings of the very **bottom notes** together. Really picture them in your head. This opens up the range of notes . . . deep and rich and fabulous. These are big personal favourites on alto and tenor.

To play the other three **bottom** notes you always have to hold bot**C** down.

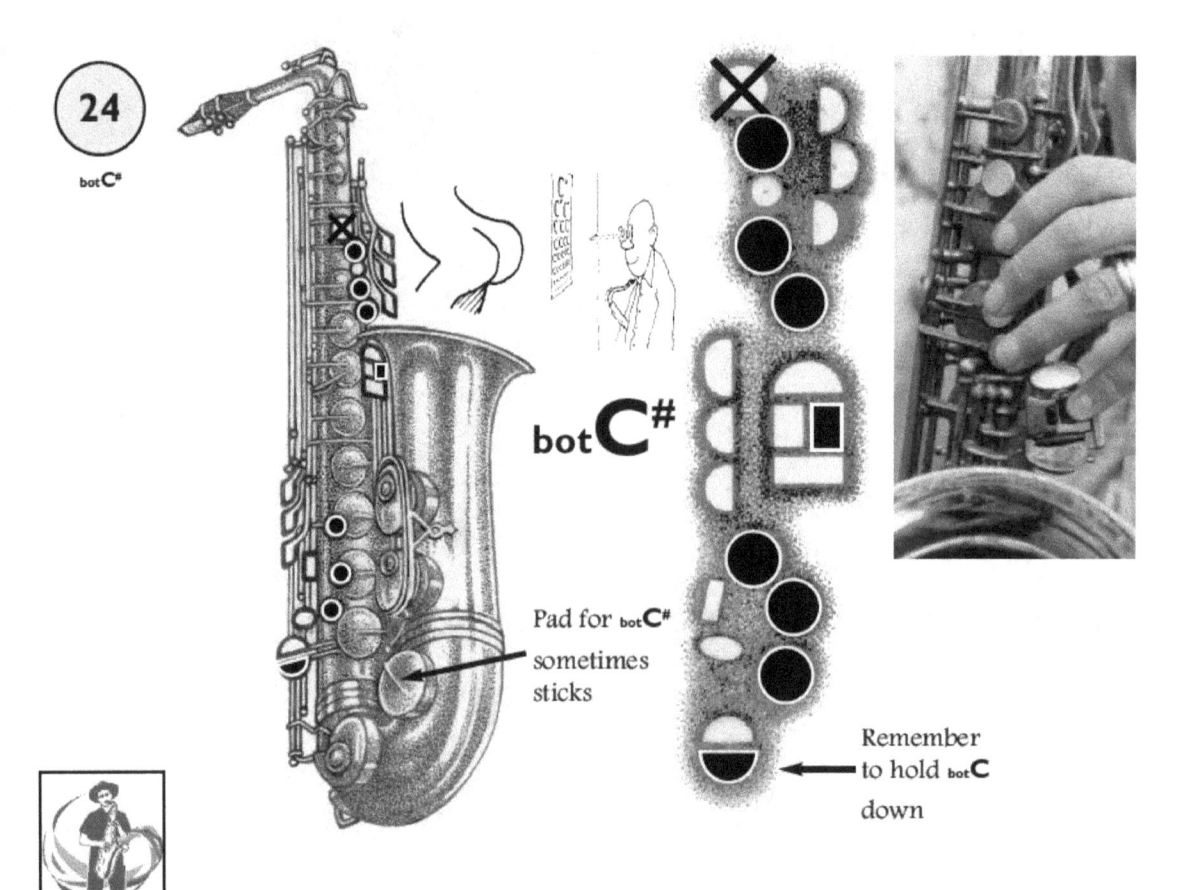

24
botC#

bot**C#**

Pad for botC# sometimes sticks

Remember to hold botC down

# CH 6 – BOTTOM B

The left-hand little finger plays the other three **bottom** notes. Press down the outside petal key (see page 162) to play botC#. For botB slide the left-hand little finger across to the inside petal key (see below).

Blow really softly and push from your guts. Tease the bottom notes out.

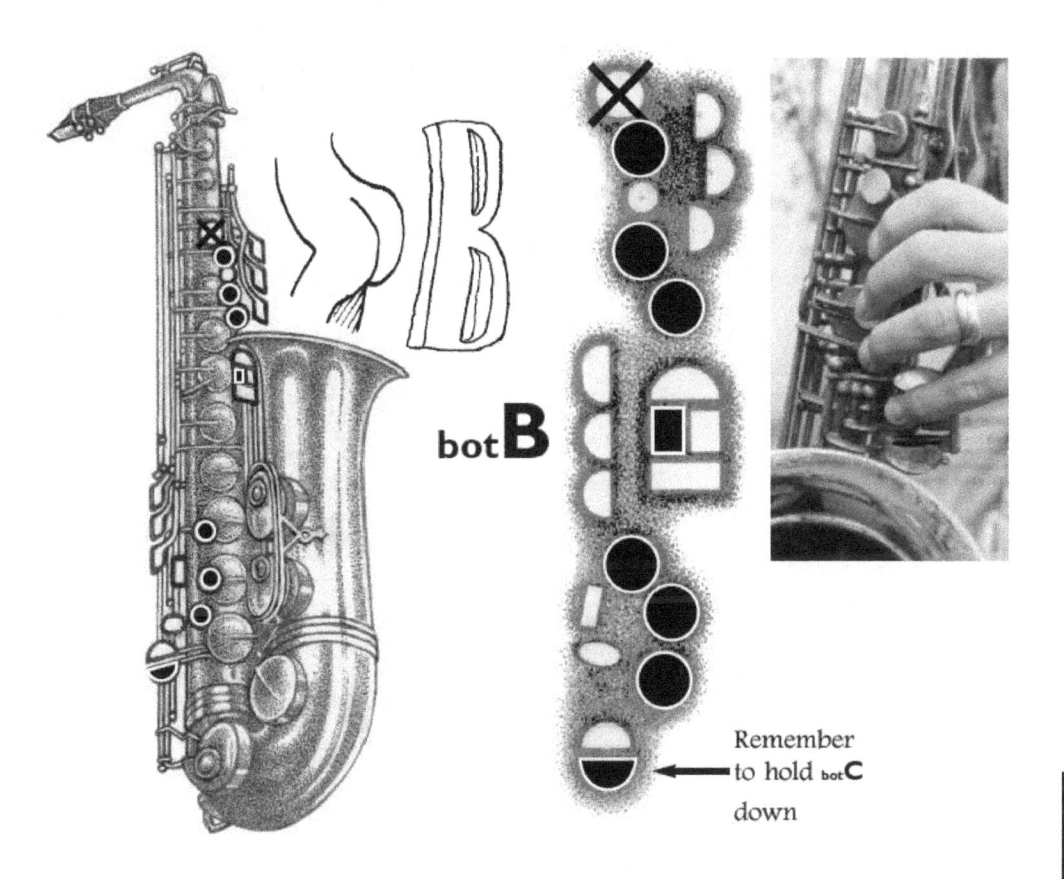

botB

25
botB

Remember to hold botC down

# 164    Ch 6 – St James Revisited

## *St James Infirmary* (revisited)

(26)

¹ ₍bot₎B D F# F# F# E F# D ₍bot₎B /

² ₍bot₎B D F# F# F# B G F# /

³ ₍bot₎B D F# F# E F# D ₍bot₎B /

⁴ ₍bot₎B D ₍bot₎B D D ₍bot₎B /

Now replay *St James Infirmary* with the addition of this verse – deep and rich.

On phrase 4 you can 'cheat' by leaving the left-hand little finger (₍bot₎B key) down. Doing this doesn't really affect the ₍bot₎B and leaves your left pinky in the correct position.

# CH 6 – BOTTOM B FLAT

165

The final and lowest note is bot**B**$^b$. This involves stretching the little finger to touch only the bottom part of the petal keys. Make sure all the other fingers are still holding down their keys as it's easy for them to slip off when you stretch the left-hand pinky. Take care to control the volume of the note. Always remember to **relax your bottom lip** and **push from your guts.**

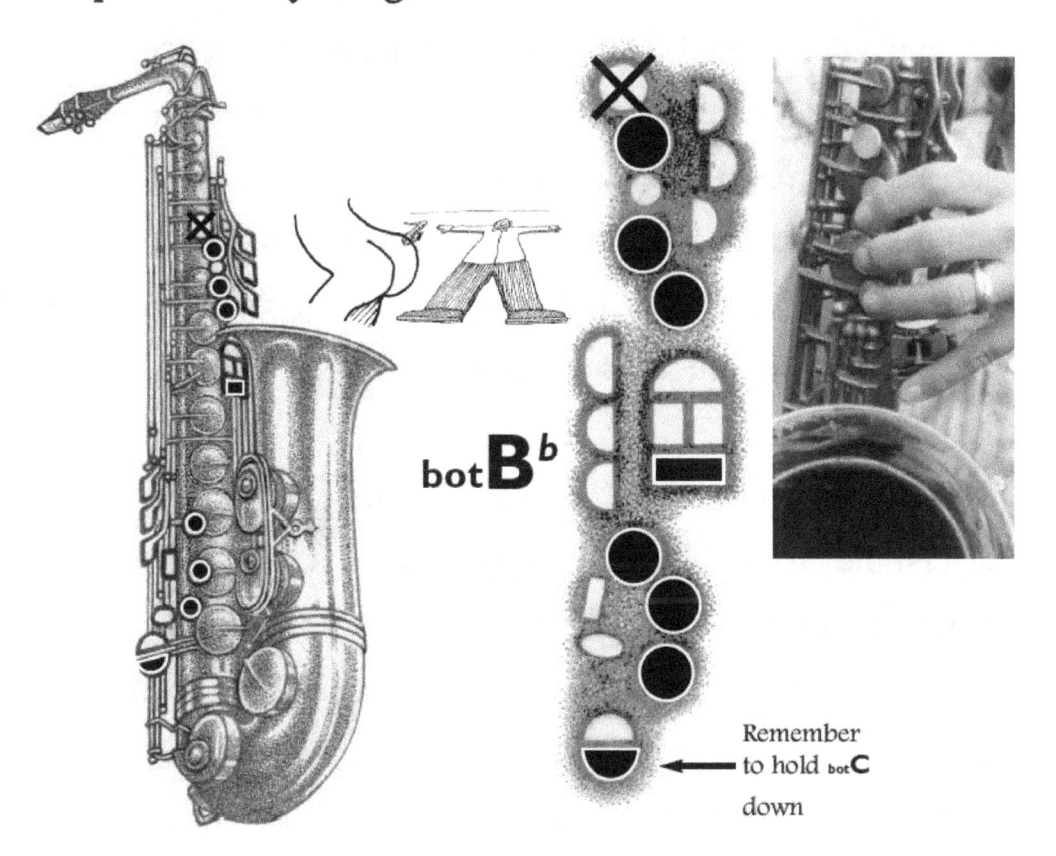

bot**B**$^b$

27

bot**B**$^b$

Remember to hold bot**C** down

# Nobody Knows the Trouble I've Seen
## traditional

Sax man Andy Hamilton was originally from Jamaica and was en route for the USA in 1949 but never got further than Birmingham, a city that he grew to love, where he married and raised 10 children. For the next 40 years he taught hundreds of students the sax and entertained thousands with a tone described by UK jazz writer John Fordham as "sumptuous, sensuous . . . and irresistible".

Then at 72, in 1991, he recorded a debut album, 'Silvershine', named after a calypso song he wrote as a young man for the action-hero actor Errol 'Robin Hood' Flynn, who hired Andy to play sax on his Caribbean yacht *Zaka*. And it was on 'Silvershine' where I first heard a soulful sax take of this gospel song.

# Nobody Knows...

Verse 1    ¹**A** bot**C D F G A A A A** / ²**A F D F E D** bot**C** /

³**A** bot**C D F** / **B**♭ **A A A A** / ⁴**C A G D F** /

Verse 2    ⁵**A** / ⁶bot**C D F G A A A A** / ⁷**A** bot**C D F F D E** bot**C** /

⁸**C A** bot**C D F** ᴳ**A A A** / ⁹**C C A G D F** /

Middle 8    ¹⁰**A C C C A** / ¹¹**A C C A** / ¹²**C A G** /

¹³**A C C A** / ¹⁴**A G F** bot**C** bot**B**♭ /

¹⁵**D E F G A G** / ¹⁶**A G F** /

Verse 3    ¹⁷**A** bot**C D F G A A** / ¹⁸**A F D A G F E D** bot**C** /

¹⁹bot**C A** bot**C D F** / ²⁰**G A A A F** /

²¹**C A G D F** / ²² bot**B**♭ bot**C** /

28    With sax

29    Without sax

The main fingering difficulty – and it is pretty similar to *What a Wonderful World* – is when we are going to land on that bot**C**. Take the air out of the horn, rather than putting the air into it, to *soften the note*.

Equally, when we play the bot$B^b$, don't foghorn it out but *ease* the note out. It's another beautiful part of the sax, a lovely rich and fruity noise – *ease* that note out.

Sing the tune along with the backing music, get it firmly ensconced in your bonce so that you really know that tune. Again, when you hear the recorded version of the saxophone being played, sing it, hum it, get the tune in your head, get the timing in your head – it's all by the ear and training your ears is the critical part of this.

Use your *imagination* to get the deepest tone possible.

Andy says of his playing, "I try to put myself and what I feel into playing . . . sometimes I feel the music coming to me, I get tears in my eyes. I can't help it. It's the emotion . . . I just play what I can. I play me."

# Ch 6 – Summary

Now try playing these **bottom** notes from botC# to botB♭ and back up again – see them all together on the next page. Now play **B blues** again from botB to (B).

While playing this medley of bottom notes, use the **rollers** so you can slide the left-hand pinky effortlessly from one note to the next. In the early days they will sound **boomingly loud** like the *Queen Mary,* but in time you should be able to play them slowly and with control. These are *beautiful* notes that should be mixed in with the rest when you're playing.

> 30
>
> botC#, botC,
> botB, botB♭
> then
> botB♭, botB,
> botC, botC#

---

## Chapter 6
*Very Bottom Notes*
### Summary

We have learned:

- botC#, botC, botB and botB♭
- Two new tunes and two old favourites

---

# Ch 6 – Very Bottom Notes

*Left Hand*

bot C#

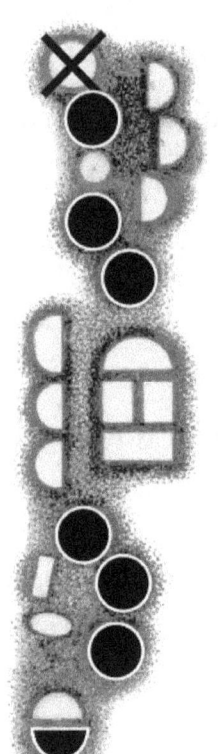

bot C

Remember: strengthen that left-hand pinky!

# Ch 6 – Very Bottom Notes

## 4 Very Bottom Notes

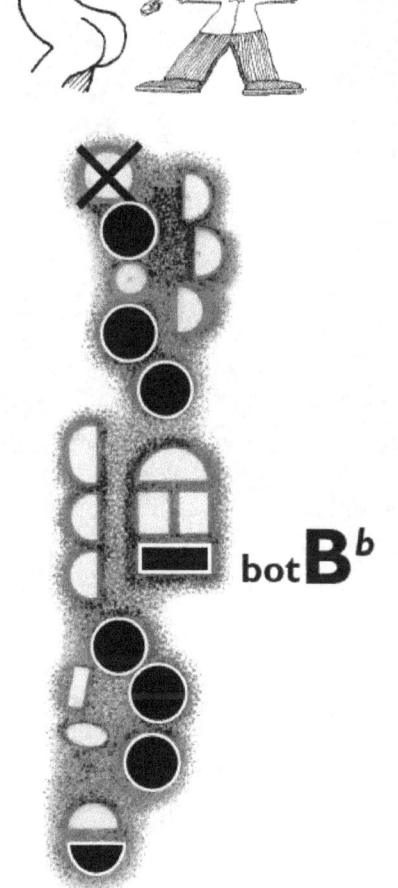

28/33

bot **B**

bot **B**$^b$

"I listen with my eyes, see with my ears, speak with my voice, and my sax."

Manu Dibango, alto sax. The Grandpappy of Makossa Soul.

## chapter seven

# Very Top Notes

Having done the bottom four notes, which now gives 28 of 33 notes, let's finish the last set – the *very top* notes. The keys used are called the **palm keys** and these notes are the real *showstoppers*.

# CH 7 – TOP D

Now, play (C#), currently your highest note. Remember to slightly *tighten up the embouchure*. This will keep the note in tune. Think of how the note will sound as this will help you achieve it. *Think high*. Blow *fast*, not hard, but fast in terms of air flow. The right-hand thumb should support the sax upright. If the horn keeps falling away to one side, and feels lopsided, then readjust the crook so it feels more balanced.

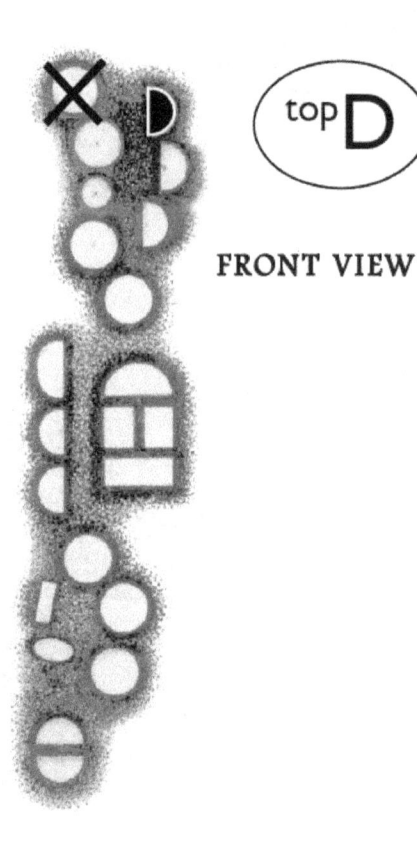

**FRONT VIEW**

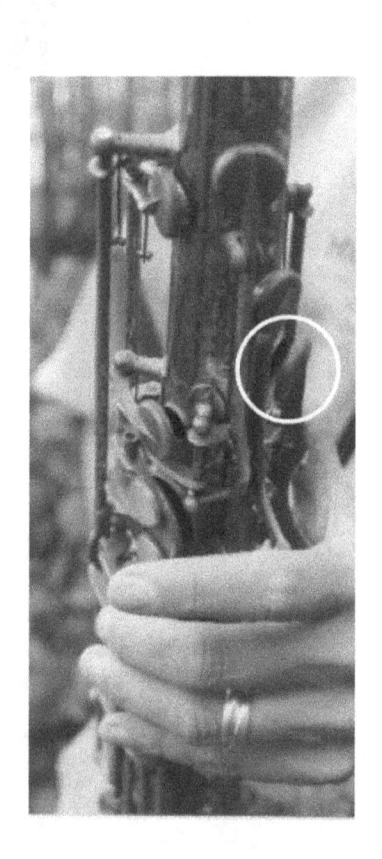

# CH 7 – TOP D

Then add the **first palm key**, (topD). Looking from the back, this key is the closest one to you. Press it down with the ball of muscle at the base of the first finger of the left hand. Rock the left hand back and forth, playing (topD) to (C#). Keep the left-hand thumb (on) the octave key. Push out with the sax.

The next step is to **rock** between (topD) and (C).

The trick here is while playing (topD) to keep the left-hand fingers hovering over the front keys. Do this in front of a mirror. Take care not to include the (C#) this time.

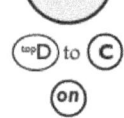

31
(topD)
(on)

32
(topD) to (C#)
(on)

33
(topD) to (C)
(on)

# Baker Street
### Gerry Rafferty/Raf Ravenscroft- (1978)

One of the most requested sax hooks is *Baker Street*. The soaring sax riding on the peak of the musical wave definitely planted the seed of desire to want to play the dream machine. The monumental alto sax riff from Raf Ravenscroft helped Gerry Rafferty's pop classic become a smash hit around the world.

Less well known is that one of Scotland-born Rafferty's early musical collaborators was comedian/actor and general wildman Billy Connolly in a group called the Humblebums.

*Baker Street*, a bit like *Careless Whisper*, comes with four separate parts to the theme, or hook as we call it. Now at the beginning, the very first phrase we are going to play of this four-phrased piece is going to start with a gliss (see page 114). Starting on (D), flip the fingers up and crash into the (top D).

# Baker Street                                             177

## *Baker Street    Original version*

1. (D) gliss↑ (topD) (C#) (B) (A) (B) (C#) (B) /
2. (D) (topD) (C#) (B) (A) (F#) /
3. (F#) (topD) (C#) (B) (A) (A) (A) (F#) /
4. (F#) (topD) (C#) (B) (A) (B) (C#) (B) /
5. (D) (topD) (C#) (B) (A) (B) /
6. (D) (topD) (C#) (B) (A) (F#) (F#) /
7. (F#) (topD) (C#) (B) (A) (A) (A) (F#) /
8. (F#) (topD) (C#) (B) (A) (B) (C#) (B) (D) (E) (D) B A B B (D) (D) (D) (F#) /

The backbone of the theme is (topD) to (C#) to (B) to (A). The thing to remember is when you go (B) (C#) it is almost like a little twitch – you hit the (B), take your finger off for (C#) and put it straight back on for the (B).

# 178

## CH 7 – 16TH TUNE

*Baker Street    Tenor version*

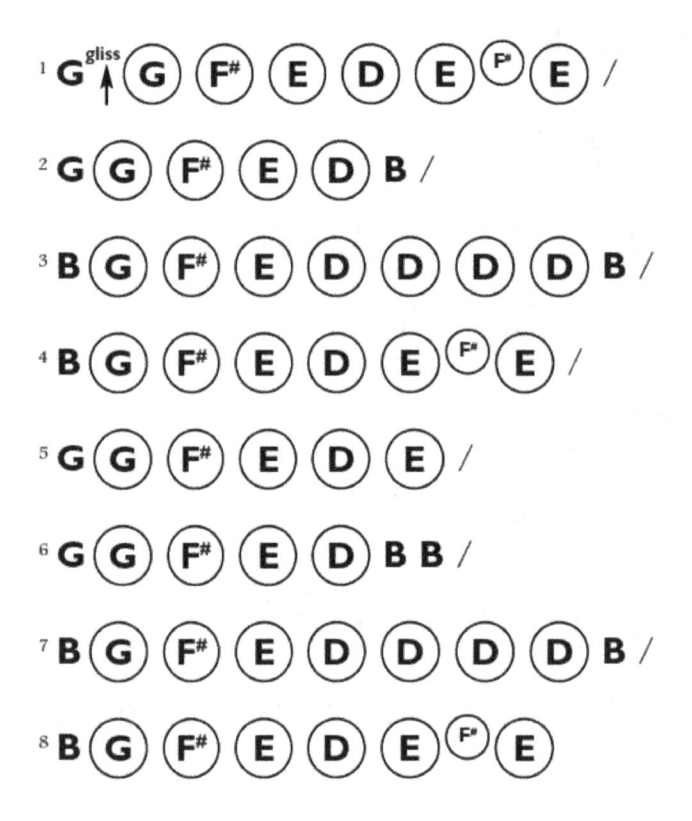

1. G^(gliss) G F# E D E (F#) E /
2. G G F# E D B /
3. B G F# E D D D B /
4. B G F# E D E (F#) E /
5. G G F# E D E /
6. G G F# E D B B /
7. B G F# E D D D B /
8. B G F# E D E (F#) E

**G A G E D E E G G B /**

Part 1min 24 secs (down an octave from the original)

This is to be played with fire – really give it what for! What a fantastic theme played by a fantastic saxophone player – what a great tune. Six minutes 40-odd seconds long, four minutes of it is sax. So that's *Baker Street*, another one to learn by ear and another one for your party tricks. Now you play *Baker Street*.

# Ch 7 – 4th Tune Revisited

We are now going to reintroduce *When the Saints*, but this time we're going to swing it. A groovy *When the Saints* was recorded by the top Hammond organist Jimmy Smith, duetting with top tenor saxman Stanley Turrentine in a sweet musical mix.

The idea of reintroducing tunes is that in theory your fingers already know the route – by moving the tunes high and low we can make them more interesting to play. We are going to play *When the Saints* with exactly the same fingering, the only difference being that instead of playing (D) with all six fingers and the thumb (**on**), we are going to play (topD). Again staccato, again very bright.

One thing you have to get used to is 'rocking' between (topD) and the lower notes. When you play (topD) keep your fingers bent round the front so that you can rock from (topD) to the (C) and from (topD) to (B) or (A) or (G), closing one note before landing on the next. Practise in front of the mirror, making sure fingers are touch tight to the keys.

# CH 7 – SAINTS REVISITED

## *When the Saints Go Marchin' In*

Verses 1 and 2   ¹ G B C (D) / ² G B C (D) /

(34) With sax   ³ G B C (D) B G B A /

⁴ B B A G G B (D) (D) C /

(35) Without sax   ⁵ B C (D) B G A G //

Verse 3   ¹¹ (G) (B) (C) (topD) / ¹² (G) (B) (C) (topD) /

¹³ (G) (B) (C) (topD) (B) (G) (B) (A) /

¹⁴ (B) (B) (A) (G) (G) (B) (topD) (topD) (C) /

¹⁵ (B) (C) (topD) (B) (G) (A) (G) /

Verse 4   ¹⁶ G B C (D) / ¹⁷ G B C (D) /

¹⁸ G B C (D) B G B A /

¹⁹ B B A G G B (D) (D) C /

²⁰ B C (D) (D#) (E) (F#) (G) /

# Ch 7 – Top D Sharp

Once you are comfortable with (topD), then with the same finger, the first of the left hand, hold the next palm key down (this is the shorter, stubbier key). This gives you (topD#).

Tighten the lip, blow fast, *think high*.

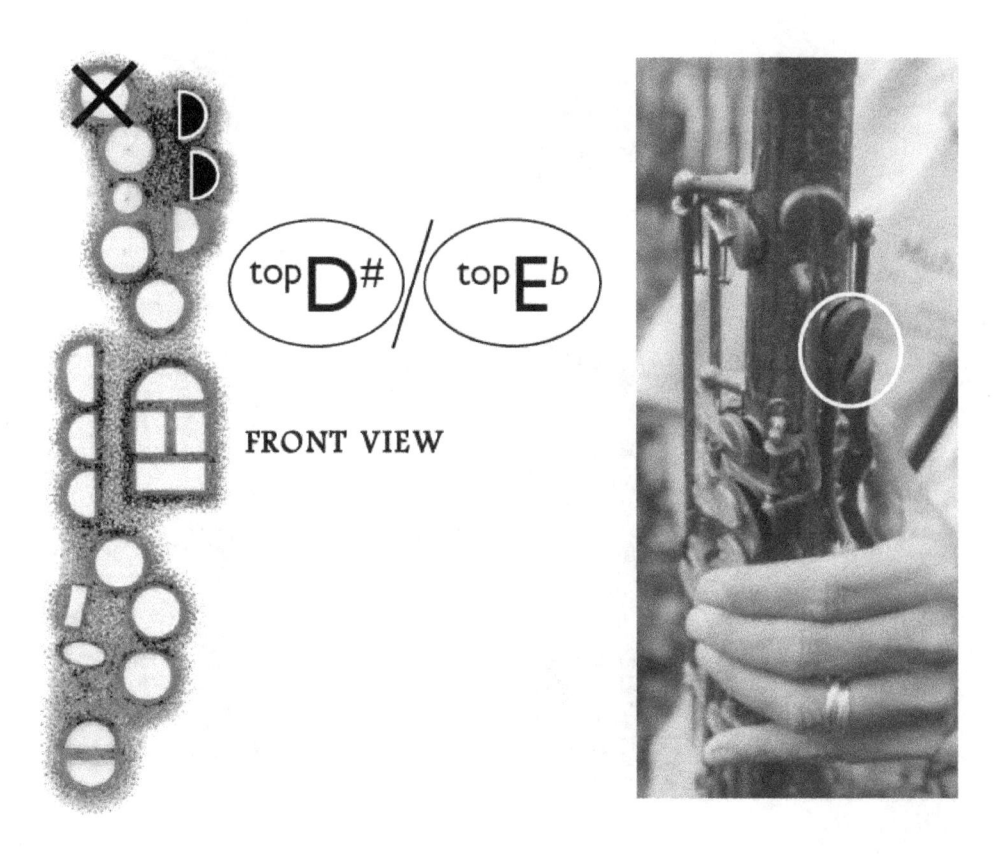

topD# / topEb

**FRONT VIEW**

# Ch 7 – Top E

**37** (topE)

**38** (topD) to (topD#) to (topE)

Holding (topD#) down, the first two palm keys, then to break up the order, Adolf cunningly added the top side key to be pressed with the right-hand first finger knuckle. This gives (topE), Mr Sax's little joke. This is one of the most difficult notes to play, so it's often easier to have a run up to (topE) by playing continuously through (topD) and (topD#) first. Tighten lip, blow fast, *think high*.

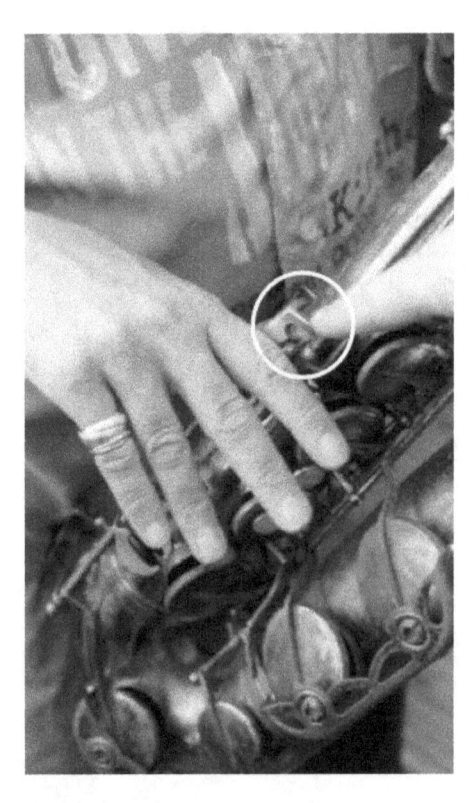

(topE)

**FRONT VIEW**

# CH 7 – TOP E

This is when your right-hand thumb, currently the only idle digit, has to play a major supporting role in keeping the sax balanced.

They do seem like a *contortionist's nightmare* (luckily great-grandad was one in a circus).

With these next songs you will have to move between (topD) and (topE) cleanly, that is without playing (topD#) sandwiched in the middle. It may seem tricky, but it's the nature of the beast.

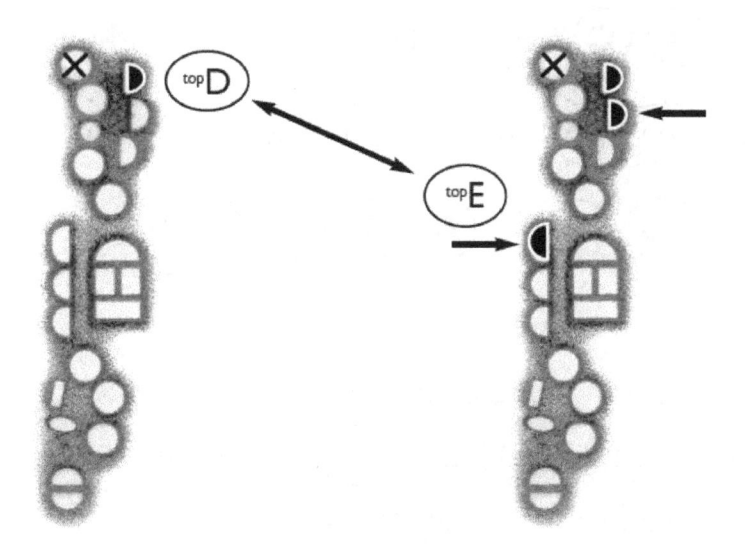

**39**
(topD) to (topE)

# 184   CH 7 – 3RD AND 2ND TUNES REVISITED

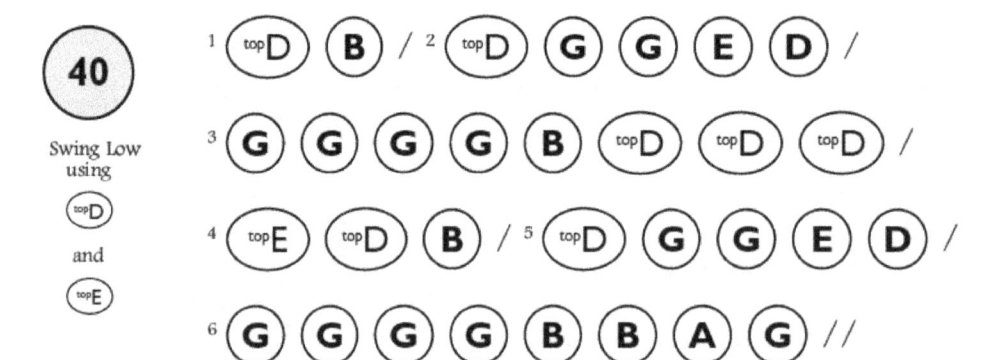

## Swing Low, Sweet Chariot

**40** — Swing Low using (topD) and (topE)

1. (topD) (B) / 2. (topD) (G) (G) (E) (D) /
3. (G) (G) (G) (B) (topD) (topD) (topD) /
4. (topE) (topD) (B) / 5. (topD) (G) (G) (E) (D) /
6. (G) (G) (G) (B) (B) (A) (G) //

## Ain't No Sunshine

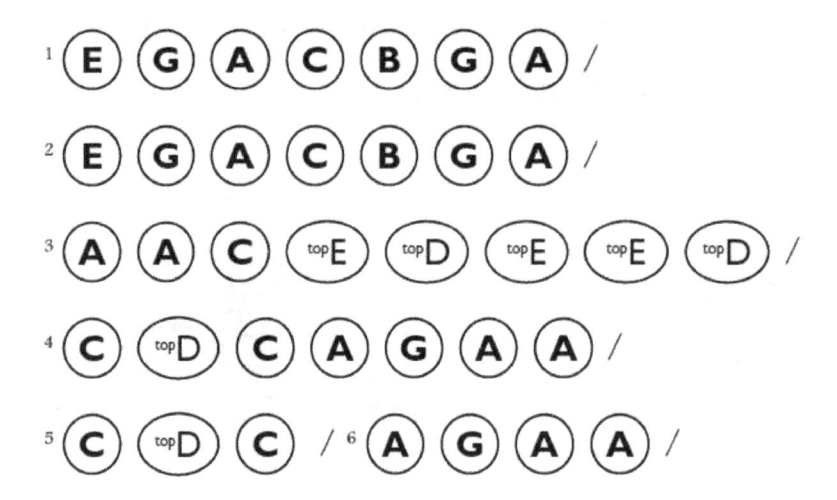

1. (E) (G) (A) (C) (B) (G) (A) /
2. (E) (G) (A) (C) (B) (G) (A) /
3. (A) (A) (C) (topE) (topD) (topE) (topE) (topD) /
4. (C) (topD) (C) (A) (G) (A) (A) /
5. (C) (topD) (C) / 6. (A) (G) (A) (A) /

Now replay *Swing Low, Sweet Chariot* and *Ain't No Sunshine* using (topD) and (topE). Try it with the backing on, mixing the lower and higher registers.

# Ch 7 - 17th Tune

# Amazing Grace
## John Newton

This is certainly one of the most spiritually moving melodies ever created. Written by an English slave captain, John Newton, in 1748 after attempting to steer the ship through a violent storm, he experienced a 'great deliverance'. He later reflected on his escape and decided God and grace had begun to work for him. Newton went on to become a minister and drew huge congregations and influenced many, among them William Wilberforce, who would one day become a successful leader in the abolishing of slavery.

Let's rescue the song from the plaintive bagpipe oblivion of the Royal Scots Dragoon Guards' version that hit number 1 in 1972. It's worth much more than that.

# 186

## CH 7 – 17TH TUNE

*Amazing Grace*

Verse 1  ¹**D G B A G B** / ²**B A G E D** /

(41) With sax

³**D G B A G B** / ⁴**A B (D)** /

⁵**B (D) B A G B** / ⁶**B A G E D** /

(42) Without sax

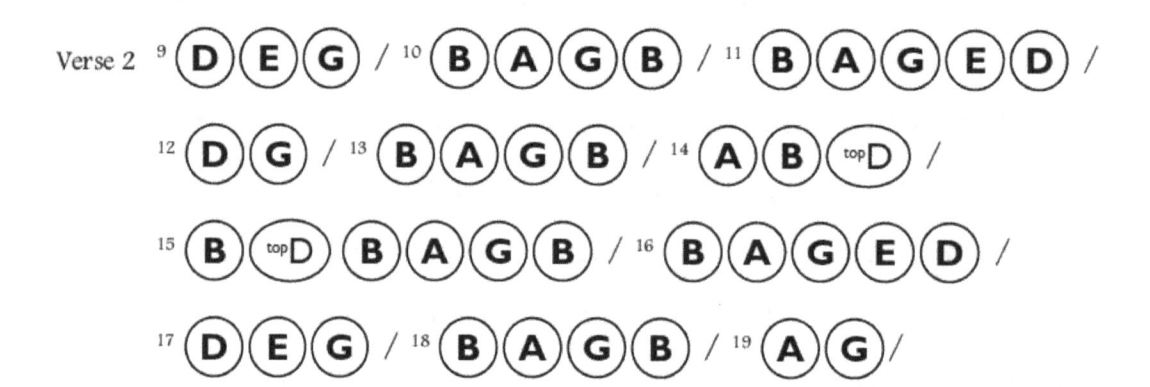

⁷**D G B A G B** / ⁸**A G** /

Verse 2  ⁹(D)(E)(G) / ¹⁰(B)(A)(G)(B) / ¹¹(B)(A)(G)(E)(D) /

¹²(D)(G) / ¹³(B)(A)(G)(B) / ¹⁴(A)(B)(topD) /

¹⁵(B)(topD)(B)(A)(G)(B) / ¹⁶(B)(A)(G)(E)(D) /

¹⁷(D)(E)(G) / ¹⁸(B)(A)(G)(B) / ¹⁹(A)(G) /

Once you've got the notes down learn it by heart. There are only five notes. In verse 3 we've just given you the key notes so try improvising around the melody. Play with, in front of and behind the piano to make your personal rendition.

# Amazing Grace

*Amazing Grace*

Verse 3  ²⁰ (D)(G) / ²¹ (B)(B) / ²² (B)(G) / ²² (E)(D) /
²³ (D)(G) / ²⁴ (B)(B) / ²⁵ (A)(topD) /
²⁶ (B)(topD)(B)(B) / ²⁷ (B)(G) / ²⁸ (E)(D) /
²⁹ (D)(G) / ³⁰ (B)(B) / ³¹ (A)(G) /


Verse 4  ³² (D)(E)(G)(E)(G) / ³³ (B)(A)(G)(B) /
³⁴ (B)(B♭)(A)(G) / ³⁵ (E)^trill(D) /
³⁶ (D)(E)(G) / ³⁷ (B)(A)(G)(B) / ³⁸ (A)(B)(topE)(topD) /
³⁹ (B)(topD)(B♭)(A)(G)(B) /
⁴⁰ (B)(B♭)(A)(G) / ⁴¹ (E)(D) /
⁴² (D)(E)(G) / ¹⁸ (B)(A)(G)(B) / ¹⁹ (A)(B♭)(A)(G) /

# Ch 7 – Top F

**43**

(topD) to (topF) with (topD#) at the end

Now finally blow through (topD), (topD#) and (topE), then adding the second finger of the left hand knuckle on the final long palm key to give you (topF).

This is almost the top note on most makes of saxophone (see diagram below). Tighten lip, blow fast, *think high*.

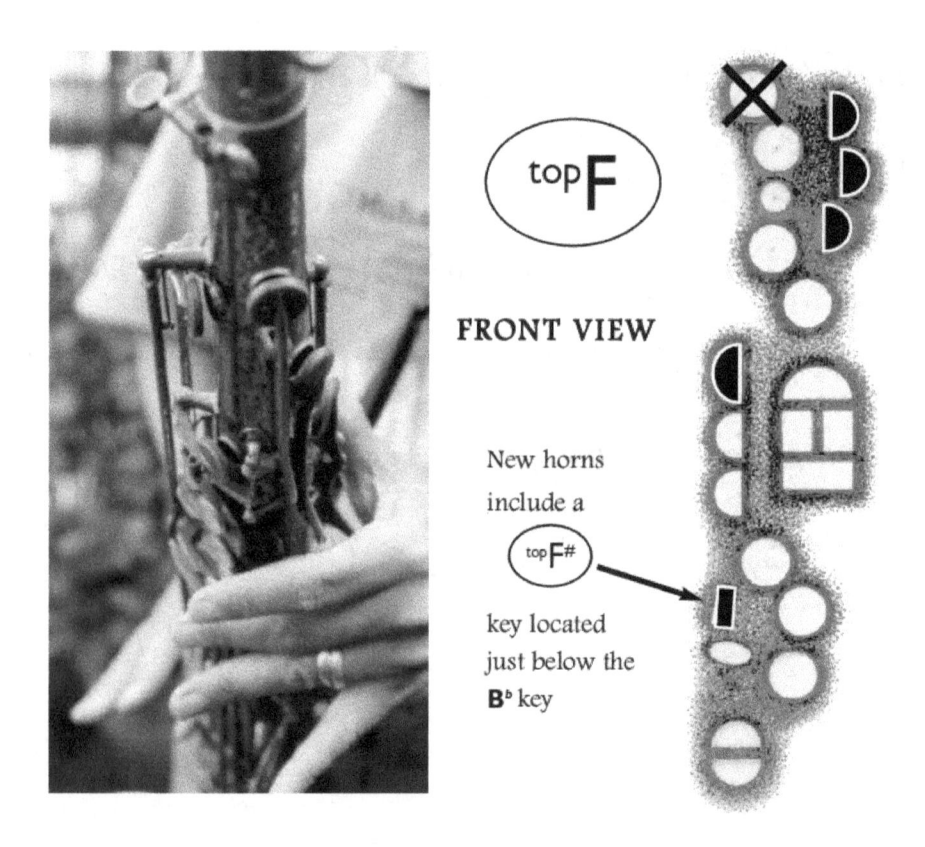

(topF)

**FRONT VIEW**

New horns include a (topF#) key located just below the B♭ key

# Ch 7 – Top F

If the note sounds a bit piercing on the ear, don't worry because later on when you're using a slightly thicker reed the tone will sound more fulsome. Play top notes up and down using the correct fingering.

(topD), (topD#), (topE) and (topF)

These are Great Notes to be used occasionally, with **devastating** results.

Imagine Dee Sharpe (topD#) trying to break through to the deaf (topDEF) man by singing high notes.

Basically, the top notes are called the same as the right hand notes.

CH 7 – 18TH TUNE

## Yesterday
### Lennon & McCartney (1965)

The birth of the song that appears in the *Guinness Book of Records* as the most covered song in history originated when 'Sir Macca' awoke with a tune flowing through his head. He stumbled to a piano and according to legend the melody fell out fully formed.

From a working title of *Scrambled Eggs*, rhyming with 'How I love your legs', a lyrical development combined with Sir George Martin's introduction of the use of acoustic and classical instruments in rock created the classic. The song was then issued as a single in the US and so outstanding was its impact that it defied American distaste for the 'highbrow' by staying at number 1 for a month.

Yesterday is the most played record ever on US radio with over 6 million airings.

# Yesterday     191

Verses 1 and 2   ¹/⁵ Yes-ter-day /

     **G  F  F  /**

²/⁶ All my trou-bles seemed so far a- way /

     **A  B  C♯  (D)  (E)  (F)(E)(D)(D) /**

³/⁷ Now it looks as though they're here to stay /

     **(D)(D)  C  B♭  A    G    B♭ A A /**

⁴/⁸ Oh, I be-lieve in yes-ter-day /

     **G  F A G  D F A A /**

Middle 8   ⁹ Why she had to go I don't know she would-n't say /

     **A  A  (D)(E)(F)(E)(D)  (E)  (D)  C  (D) A /**

¹⁰ I said some-thing wrong now I long for yes-ter-day    /

     **A A  (D)  (E)  (F)  (E)(D)(E)(D) C  (E)(F) C B♭ A/**

Verse 3  *As for Verse 1, with an extra line at the end:*

Ooh ooh ooh ooh ooh ooh /

     **F A G D F A A /**

We can do this one normally, as above, or we can do it unbelievably *high*, an octave above . . .

# 192     CH 7 – 18TH TUNE

## *Yesterday*

Verses 1 and 2   ¹/⁵ Yes-ter-day /

(G) (F) (F) /

²/⁶ All my trou-bles seemed so far a- way /

(A) (B) (C#) (topD) (topE) (topF) (topE) (topD) (topD) /

³/⁷ Now it looks as though they're here to stay /

(topD) (topD) (C) (B♭) (A) (G) (B♭) (A) (A) /

⁴/⁸ Oh, I be-lieve in yes-ter-day /

(G) (F) (A) (G) (D) (F) (A) (A) /

Middle 8   ⁹ Why she / ¹⁰ had to go I don't know

(A) (A) / (topD) (topE) (topF) (topE) (topD) (topE)

she would-n't say /

(topD) (C) (topD) (A) /

¹¹ I said / ¹² some-thing wrong now I long

(A) (A) / (topD) (topE) (topF) (topE) (topD) (topE)

for yes- ter- day       /

(topD) (C) (topE) (topF) (C) (B♭) (A) /

Verse 3   *As for Verse 1, with an extra line at the end:*

(F) (A) (G) (D) (F) (A) (A) /

# Ch 7 – Quick Top F

The mysterious Illegal Key that you have never touched in your musical career so far is now going to be used for the first time as your embouchure is now developed enough to try this.

By legalising this differently shaped key you are going to have the opportunity of playing (topF) another way. This is called *Quick* (topF) Some of the older vintage makes of saxophone don't have this key and don't therefore have this option.

**Quick**

(topF)

Now to play this, put the finger on **C** and the first finger of the left hand on the Illegal Key. While stretching the first two fingers apart, tilt the horn forward, blow fast and tighten the bottom lip. *Think high.* Have at least a No. 2½ strength on, because a thinner reed won't take the pressure from your bottom lip.

# CH 7 – QUICK TOP E

This gives you a direct route from **C** to (topF) without using the palm keys. Should Quick (topF) not sound, play the normal palm key version and keep how the note sounds in your head. Then try the Quick (topF) again with this sound firmly in your mind. *Think it.* Keep trying this until it works.

**Quick (topE)**

Once you can play Quick (topF) add the ring finger of the left hand on the **G** key as well. This gives you Quick (topE). At the beginning play Quick (topF) first and then the Quick (topE).

Be patient! This way of playing these top show-off notes is both easier on the fingers and fantastic for inserting the top notes in your playing a lot more often.

# CH 7 – 33RD NOTE: F SHARP

*195*

All modern saxophones may have the luxury of a (top F#) key. You can play this either using the Quick (top F) and adding the rectangle key or you can play (top F) the normal way using the palm keys and side key and using the third finger of the right hand to press it down. This new note is really up in the clouds.

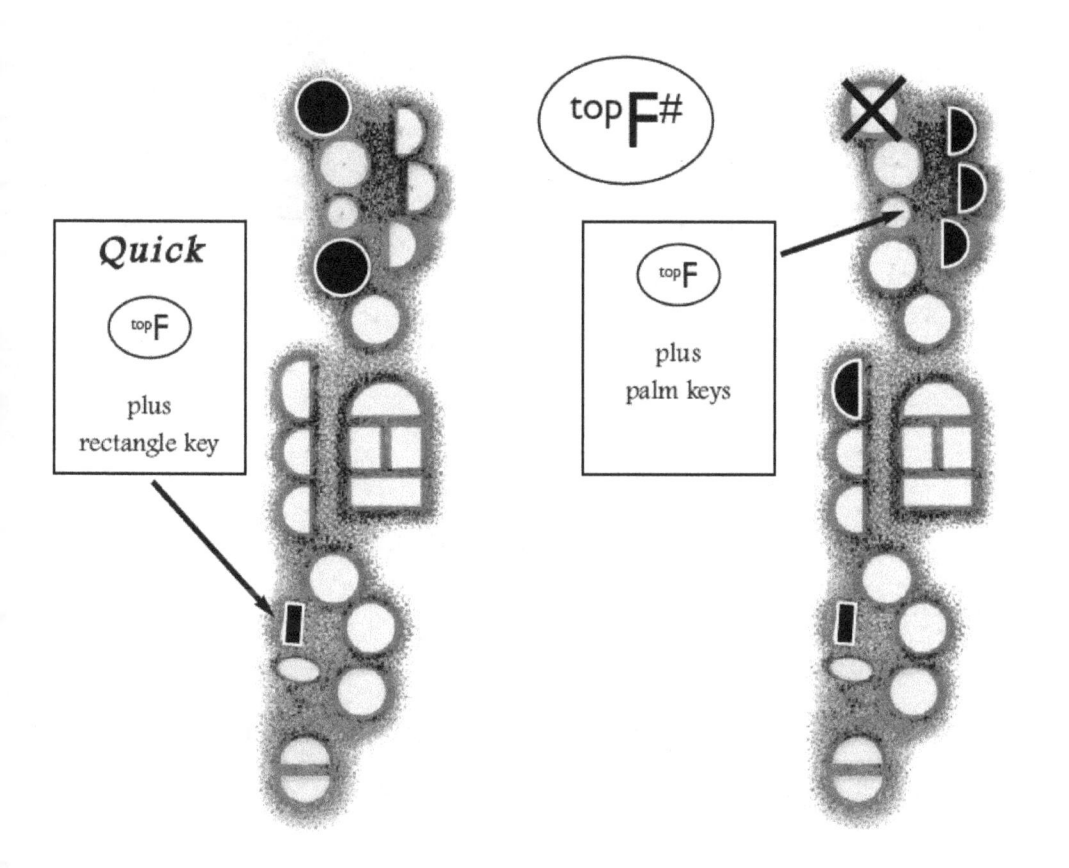

# Ch 7 – 33rd Note: F Sharp

For those without the extra key, another way of playing (topF#) is to use the Quick (topF) and add the bottom side key.

*Quick* (topF#)

Now you have 33 notes! Armed with your new note, use it in all the relevant Blues and Major and Minor keys, such as the B Blues on page 118.

At the very early stages of playing the very top notes don't tongue them. Use inflections like **woos** (see page 102) when you get full control of the notes, then try your tonguing.

Once you have mastered this version using all the top notes, you are well on your way to being an accomplished saxophonist.

Remember we have *only* got 33 notes on the sax and if you compare that to a piano that isn't a lot of notes, **so no**

# Ch 7 – Very Top Notes

**avoidance policy.** This is every note from the very bottom note to the very top. You must develop an *ear* for how each and every single note sounds.

These top and very bottom notes can be very effective and possess a sweet cutting edge. Keep persevering to get them right. Keep your embouchure correct and your breathing controlled and the notes will sing out with maximum impact.

Now you can blow from bot$B^b$ to (top$F^\#$). In the next chapter, we are going to put all the notes in a colourful order called the **Chromatics**.

---

## Chapter 7
*Very Top Notes*
### Summary
We have learned:

- (topD), (topD#), (topE), (topF) and (topF#)
- Four new tunes and three old favourites

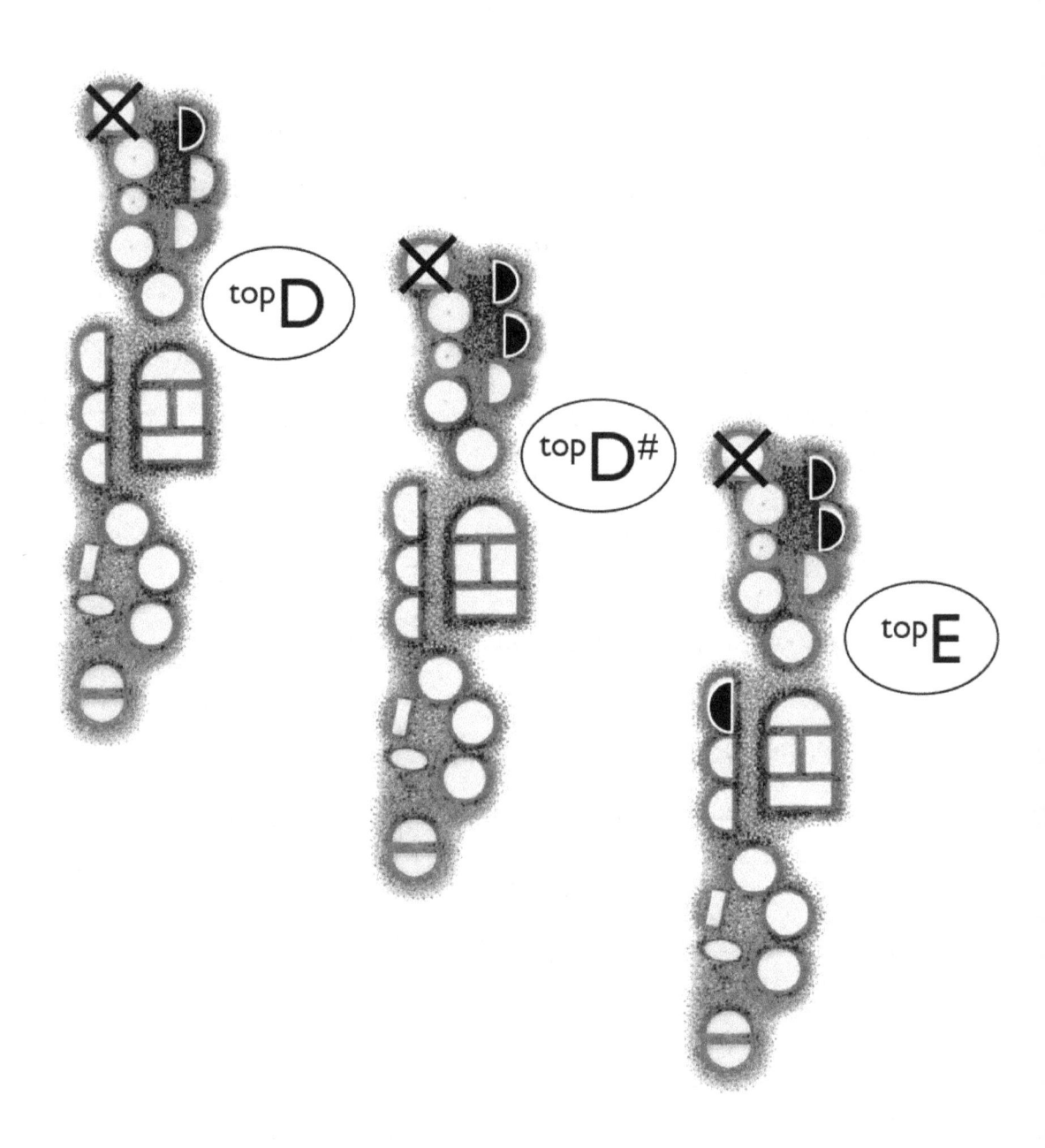

## CH 7 – VERY TOP NOTES

# CH 7 – VERY TOP NOTES

# 5 Very Top Notes

33/33

top F

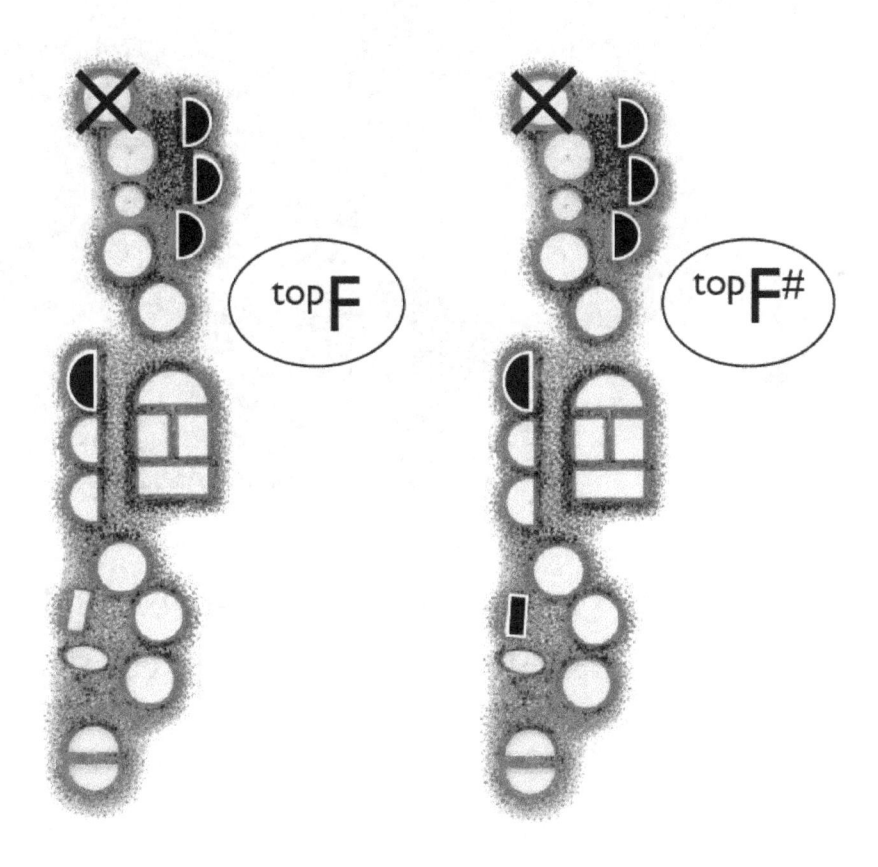

top F#

*200*

"I'm going to blow this goddamn horn 'til they lay it down on top of me."

Ben Webster

## chapter eight

# The Chromatics
## – the colourful scale

**C**hrome means colour and this is the most colourful set of notes of all. What we are going to do here, is set the naturals, the four sharps and B flat and show how they live side by side on the saxophone.

# CH 8 – UP AND DOWN THE LADDER

**44**
D - D# - E

**45**
E - F - F#

**46**
D D# E F F#
Up/down, right hand

**47**
G G# A

**48**
A B♭ B

**49**
C C# (D)

**50**
F# G G# A B♭
B C C# (D)
Left hand notes

Playing the Chromatics is like *running* up and down a ladder, stepping on **every** rung, on the way up and on the way back down.

The best way of approaching chromatics is to separate the hands. So let's start by concentrating on the **right hand**. Have a look at the chart on the following pages for these notes. Starting on **D**, octave key **off**, play **D#** and then **E** and back down again. Once you can play this smoothly, try **E**, **F** and **F#**. Now play these five chromatic notes going up and down, all in one go. Note that as we go up the sax, the sharps are always *after* the naturals.

**Left hand** now. The next three *'rungs'* up are **G**, **G#** and **A**. Again, get this combination slick and then move up to **A**, **B♭** and **B**, then to **C** and on to **C#** and (**D**). Now play these eight notes together, going up and down the ladder.

# CH 8 – UP AND DOWN THE LADDER

Once you are comfortable with each hand, put them together and play these dozen chromatic notes slowly from **D** up to (**D**). What a sleek phrase! Now, with the octave key (**on**), carry on running up the ladder, playing every single note, from (**D**) to (**top D**).

Now let's go down from (**top D**). Remember that on the way down the sharps come *before* the naturals. So this time we will start with the left hand first (the main *pivotal* hand), octave key (**on**). The first note is (**C#**) to (**C**), then *The Switch* to (**B**) and then (**B♭**), finishing with (**A**) to (**G#**) to (**G**).

If you have any problems, break up the phrases and work on each combination separately.

**51**
D D# E F F#
G G# A B♭ B
C C# (D)
Lower register

**52**
(D) (D#) (E)
(F) (F#) (G)
(G#) (A) (B♭)
(B) (C) (C#)
(top D)
Upper register

**53**
(top D)
(C#) (C) (B)
(B♭) (A) (G#)
(G)

44-49

# 204    Ch 8 – The Chromatics

*Left Hand*

When you go **down**...

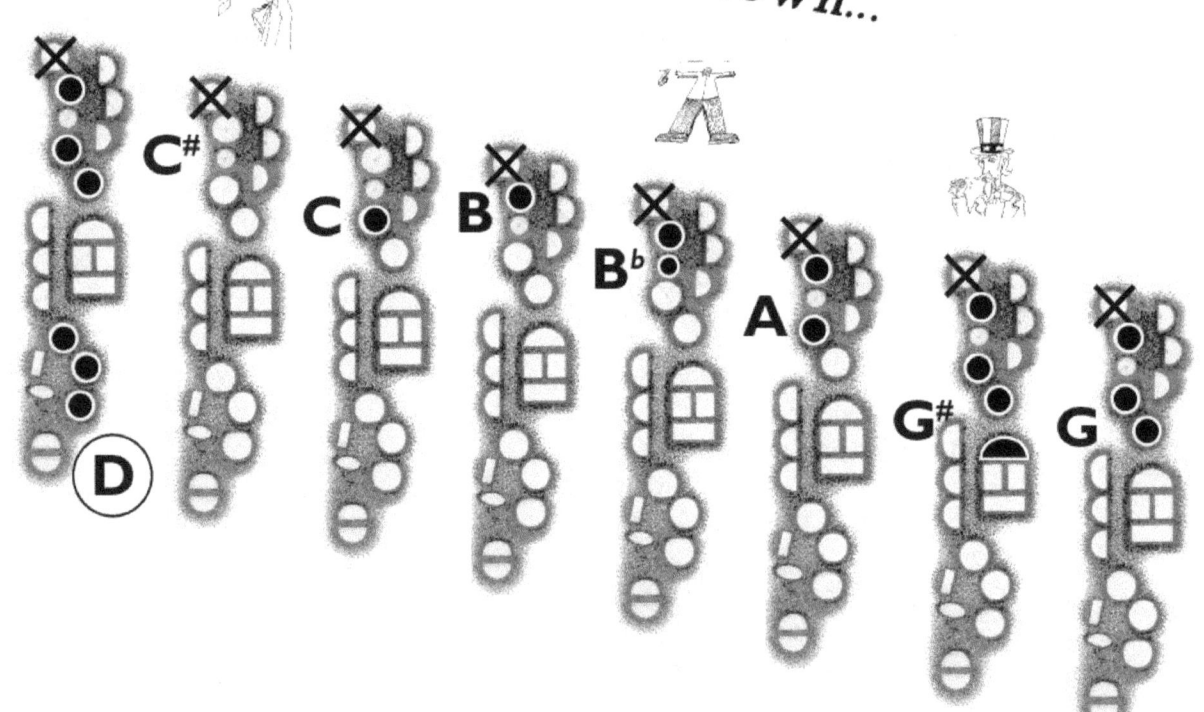

D, C#, C, B, B♭, A, G#, G

When you go **up**...
the Sharps come **after** the Naturals

CH 8 – THE CHROMATICS  205

# The Main Chromatic Notes  33/33

*the Sharps come **before** the Naturals*

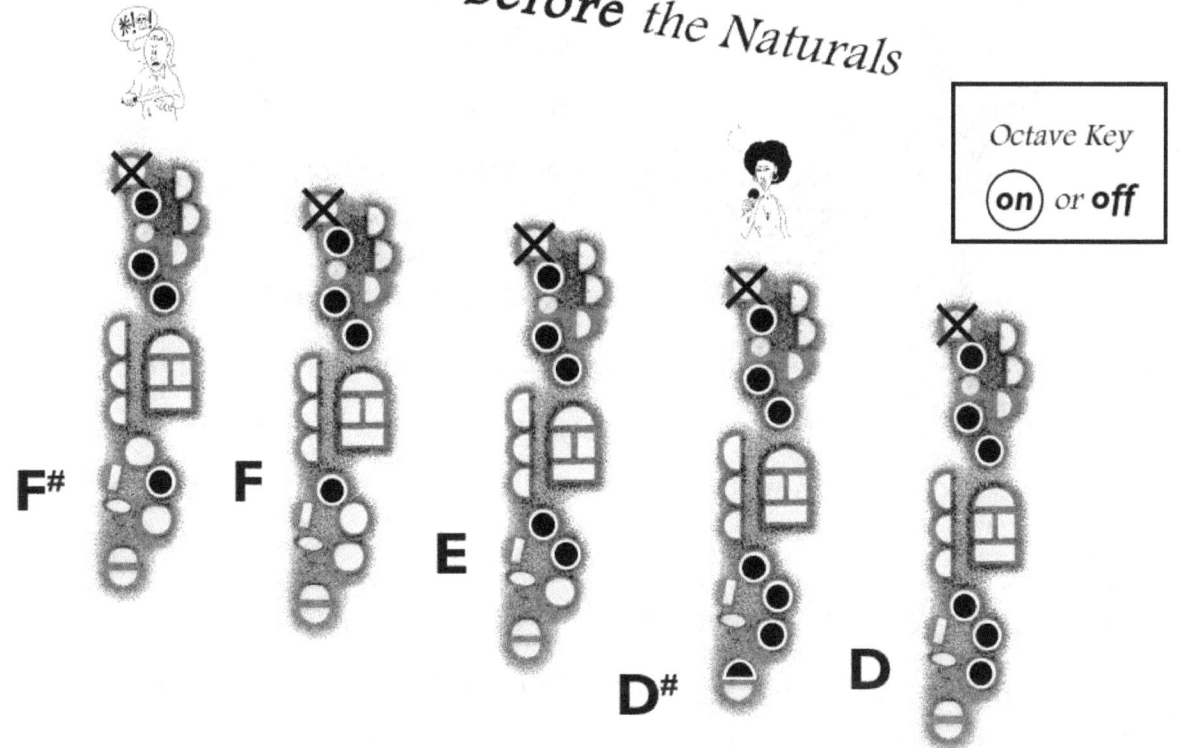

Octave Key **on** or **off**

F#   F   E   D#   D

Right Hand

# Ch 8 – Learn It By Heart

**54**
G F# F
E D# D

For the right hand going down, play **G** **F#** to **F**, add the **E**, then the **D#** to the **D**.

**55**
Top **D** to lower **D** in two gulps

Once again, when you are comfortable with each hand, put them together and play these notes slowly downwards, starting on **top D** down to **D**. Now take the thumb **off** the octave key and carry on running down, playing every single note, from **C#** to **D**.

**56**
Low **D** to top **D** in one gulp!

**57**
Top **D** to low **D** in one gulp!

To celebrate being able to play the chromatics, why not show off your new skills by running from **D** all the way up to **top D** in one huge active gulp of air – 24 superbly crafted notes in one colossal breath. Likewise, do the same masterful run going back down. Hooray! 24 notes – that's two whole octaves on the saxophone.

# Ch 8 – Learn It By Heart

Do this slowly. Do this quickly. Memorise it! You can work on perfecting your fingers playing the chromatic runs in front of the TV. It is like walking up the piano hitting every note in order as they come. The difference on the sax is that it is all from feel and touch.

We can't stress how important this is. It's probably the most important thing shown to you so far – something we want you to learn by heart and do every single time you warm up. This will get all your fingers working and is wonderfully flamboyant to boot.

## Pink Panther
### Henry Mancini (1963)

So here's your next party piece, Henry Mancini's *Pink Panther*. The instant hook from Mancini and Plas Johnson's spellbinding tenor sax sound make this the number 1 popular sax gem, the most requested piece at the Blowout Sax School. When we wrote to Johnson for a top learning tip, he said, "Play it 500 times. It always sounds better then."

The *Pink Panther* uses the notes from the **F# blues** scale, so get comfortable with these notes before you play the tune.

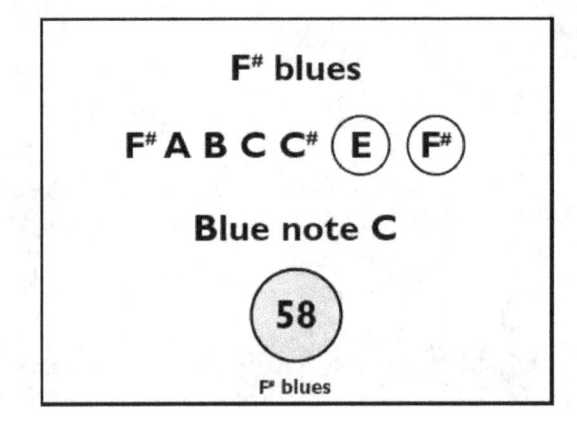

---

**F# blues**

F# A B C C# (E) (F#)

**Blue note C**

(58)

F# blues

# Pink Panther

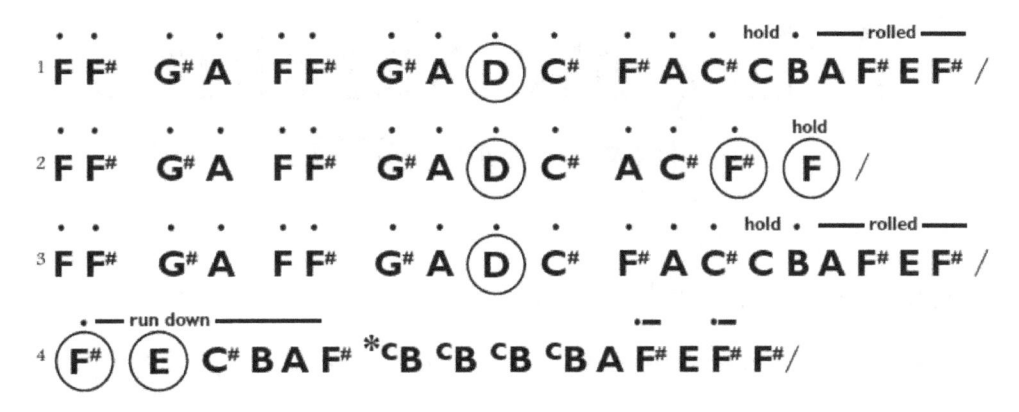

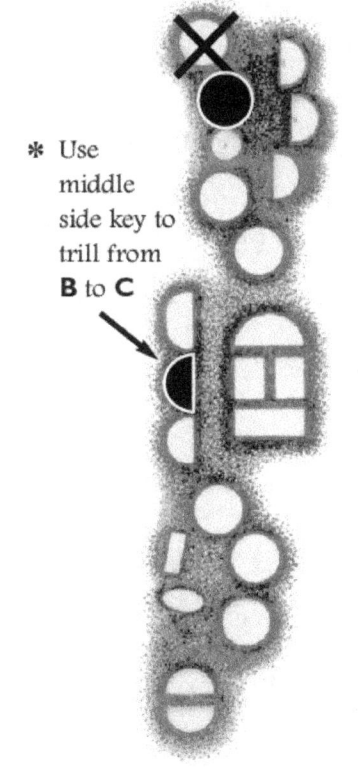

$^1$ **F F**♯ **G**♯ **A  F F**♯ **G**♯ **A** (**D**) **C**♯  **F**♯ **A C**♯ **C B A F**♯ **E F**♯ /

$^2$ **F F**♯ **G**♯ **A  F F**♯ **G**♯ **A** (**D**) **C**♯  **A C**♯ (**F**♯) (**F**) /

$^3$ **F F**♯ **G**♯ **A  F F**♯ **G**♯ **A** (**D**) **C**♯  **F**♯ **A C**♯ **C B A F**♯ **E F**♯ /

$^4$ (**F**♯) (**E**) **C**♯ **B A F**♯ *****C**B **C**B **C**B **C**B **A F**♯ **E F**♯ **F**♯ /

$^5$ **A F**♯ **E F**♯ **F**♯ /$^6$ **A F**♯ **E F**♯ **F**♯ /$^7$ (**G**♯) ↓

\* Use middle side key to trill from **B** to **C**

Play it slowly to overcome its trickiness, bearing in mind that two thirds of the tune is the opening phrase. Get this under your fingers. Remember that the notes with dots above them are short staccato. Gradually speed it up as it's quicker than you think.

On phrase 4, you can use a short cut from **B** to **C**, another one of Adolphe Sax's cunning little designs. Put your finger on the **B** and nudge the middle side key. So now play the *Pink Panther*, learn it by heart and enjoy it!

# Bring Me Sunshine
## Jack Greene (1969)

Eric Morecambe and Ernie Wise are a British comedy institution whose sense of the ridiculous and magical rapport drew huge audiences. *Bring Me Sunshine*, their wonderfully happy theme tune – which was a hit for legendary Country and Western singer Willie Nelson in 1969 – has got two or three lovely little chromatic phrases.

The hardest bit is when you bring the tempo and the pace up, you've got to keep the chromatic lick fast. It's got to be slick. Those are the two bits to work on and that is why we are playing *Bring Me Sunshine*.

Eric Morecambe once said, " There is no such thing as an original to start with. You start by copying and once you've built up confidence and worked hard enough, the real person begins to come out." This applies equally to music.

# Bring Me Sunshine

**211**

¹/⁹Bring me sun-shine / ²/¹⁰In your smile /

    C   B A  E  /  C  B  A  /

³/¹¹Bring me laugh-ter / ⁴/¹²All the while /

    C   B A  F  /  C  B  A  /

⁵/¹³In this world where we live /

  (E)(D#)(D)  C  B B♭ /

⁶/¹⁴There should be more hap-pi-ness /

  G  G#  A F  A (E)(D)/

⁷/¹⁵So much joy you can give /

  (E)(D#)(D) C B A  /

⁸/¹⁶To each brand new bright to-mor-row /

  B C (E) (D)(E) (G)(E)(D)/

¹⁷Bring me fun / ¹⁸Bring me sun-shine /

  C  B A F/ (D) C B  G  /

¹⁹Bring me lo- ve /

  (E)  (E)(E) C /

The more you play and listen and get to know tunes inside out, both lyrically and melodically, the more your confidence and tone and beauty of playing will grow.

## When I'm Sixty Four
### Lennon & McCartney (1967)

The gifted genius Paul McCartney wrote this picture-postcard music hall number when he was a teenager. Lennon & McCartney are probably the most celebrated songwriting partnership of all time, yet neither could read or write a note of music – proving that there is **no** obstacle to music making.

This song is ideal for improving your chromatic skills. You will find, as in most tunes, a few tricky phrases. We have set aside two, phrases 3 and 4. One **really** good way of working out harder phrases is:
Don't be tempted to play your two times slow too fast. Slow it

### "two times slow, one time fast"

right down. Slow means slow. Then try it one time fast. A couple of these and you will be well on your way to mastering those phrases that make you want to pull your hair out.

# When I'm Sixty Four

¹When I get old-er los-ing my hair / ²Man-y years from now /

**E   D♯E  G E G  A G C  /  C  Ⓔ C   A  Ⓓ /**

³Will you still be send-ing me a Val-en-tine /

**B   B Ⓓ Ⓓ  B  B Ⓓ Ⓓ B B♭ A /**

⁴Birth-day greet-ings bot-tle of wine /

**B   C  C♯   Ⓓ Ⓔ Ⓓ♯ Ⓓ  C /**

⁵If I'd been out till quart-er to three / ⁶Would you lock the door /

**E D♯ E   G E G   A G C  /  Ⓔ   Ⓔ Ⓓ A C /**

⁷Will you still need me / ⁸Will you still feed me /

**C   A  C  Ⓓ♯ Ⓓ /  C  A C B A /**

⁹When I'm six- ty four /

**Ⓔ   Ⓔ Ⓔ Ⓔ C /**

¹⁰Ev-ery sum-mer we can rent a cot-tage on the Isle of Wight /

**C A C A  C A C A C  A  C A C F G /**

If it's not too dear/ ¹¹You'll be ol- der too /

**G E  G A E  /  A   B C Ⓖ Ⓔ /**

¹²And if you say the wo-r-d /

**Ⓔ Ⓓ C Ⓓ Ⓓ A       /**

¹²I could stay with you /

**C/ A / G / A / C /**

## Girl from Ipanema
### De Moraes, Gimbel, Jobin (1964)

Welcome to the "beautiful luxurious sound" of Stan Getz's tenor sax where his playing of the Bossa Nova, often accompanied by the lilt of Astrud Gilberto's voice, will beguile and transport the listener straight to a beach in Rio. "His phrases hung in the air like wreathes of smoke." – David Gelly

This neatly brings us to the subject of **smoking**. As long as you breathe properly, smoking will not play a major part in blowing. Having said that, smoking is bad for your longterm saxophone career and your general health.

# Girl from Ipanema

An icon who would light a cigarette as he started singing in concert was Frank Sinatra. His version of *Girl from Ipanema* was as dreamy, cool and sexy as you could hear.

'The Voice' was a man who didn't know any theory and barely sightread, but his *instincts* were impeccable – the best, perhaps, of any singer of the 20th century. Part of it was song selection, part style, part sheer chops. And he kept it up for decades, changing sounds, changing his very voice, always setting the standards in style and performance . . . he *was* 20th-century popular singing. And – like Elvis, Lennon & McCartney, Louis Armstrong, Irving Berlin – it shows there is nothing to stop anyone playing and creating music.

By the same token, the supreme musical innovator – Miles 'Prince of Darkness' Davis – tells us his gifted secret. "I love the way Sinatra sings . . . if you want to know the real truth. I learned to phrase from listening to all his early records. So now you know."

## Ch 8 – 22nd Tune

### Girl from Ipanema

Verse 1   ¹Tall and tanned and young and love-ly /

**C  / A A   G  C   A A A /**

²The girl from Ip-an-em-a goes walk-ing and when she pas-ses /

**G  C  A   A G C C A  A   A G B♭   G G G /**

³Each one she pas-ses goes 'Aah' /

**F  A  F  F  F  D#  F  /**

Verse 2   ⁴When she walks she's like a Sam-ba that swings so cool and sways so gent-ly /

**C   A A  G  C A A A G  C   A A G  C   A A A /**

⁵That when she pas-ses /

**G  B♭  G  G G /**

⁶Each one she pas-ses goes 'Aah' /

**F  A  F  F  F  D#  F  /**

Try out **legato** on *Girl from Ipanema*. When you use the tongue on the repeated notes, especially in phrase 7, sing the tune in your head so the effect of the legato actually matches the phrasing of the tune.

This is one of the hardest tunes. The tonguing with the **C,** the **G** and the **A** in the intro is no problem, just keep the

# Girl from Ipanema

## *Girl from Ipanema*

Bridge  ⁷Oh but he watch~es so sad~ly /

B♭ B B♭ G♯  B♭ G♯ F♯ G♯ /

⁸How can he tell her he loves her /

C♯ (D) C♯ B C♯ B A B /

⁹Yes he would give his heart glad~ly /

(D) (D♯) (D) C (D) C B♭ C /

¹⁰But each day when she walks to the sea /

(D) (D♯) (F) F G A B♭ C C♯ /

¹¹She looks straight a~head not at me /

(D) (D♯) D♯ F G A B♭ B /

Verse 3  ¹²Tall and tanned and young and love~ly /

C A A  G C A A A /

¹³The girl from Ip~an~em~a goes walk~ing /

G C A A G C C A A A /

¹⁴And when she pas~ses he smiles but she does~n't see. //

G (D) B♭ B♭ B♭ G (F) G A A G A //

tune rhythmically flowing in your head. When you get to the bridge in phrase 7 (when the melody changes), there is a **sequential pattern**. There are three of the same types of

# Ch 8 – 22nd Tune

sequential patterns in the first part (phrases 8, 9 and 10) and two at the end (phrases 11 and 12). Those phrases are exactly the same but with different notes, so concentrate on your notes like mad. Likewise the last two phrases are exactly the same as well.

Do it slowly, get it right, get it accurate and then build up as quickly as possible. Think of Rio, think of somewhere warm, keep the tune in your head.

CH 8 – 23RD TUNE

# The Entertainer
**Scott Joplin (1902)**

Ragtime was the Rock 'n Roll of the 1900s, with newspapers attacking its jagged rhythms for "producing insanity . . . 90% of insane asylum inmates love ragtime," (*New York Times*, 2 October 1911), and complaining that "ragtime is not music it is a disease – Famous Doctor". For many, this infectious and joyful style of music was first heard on the 1970s movie soundtrack to *The Sting*.

The greatest composer of rags was Scott Joplin, who also went on to write an opera, *Treemonisha*, on the subject of the liberation of the black race. The project failed to take off and ironically Joplin was put in a lunatic asylum before dying a premature death in 1917.

Joplin would have been proud that ragtime was at the start of a type of music – Jazz – that would change the world.

# 220

## CH 8 – 23RD TUNE

### *The Entertainer*

Verse 1 and 2  ¹/⁸ D D# E C E C E C / ²/⁹ C (D)(D#)(E) C (D)(E) B (D) C /

**59** With sax  ³/¹⁰ D D# E C E C E C / ⁴/¹¹ A G F# A C (E) (D) C A (D) /

⁵/¹² D D# E C E C E C / ⁶/¹³ C (D)(D#)(E) C (D)(E) B (D) C /

**60** Without sax  ⁷/¹⁴ C(D)(E) C(D)(E) C(D)C(E)C(D)(E)

C(D)C(E)C(D)(E) B (D) C //

Middle 8 / bridge  ¹⁵ E F F# G A G / ¹⁶ E F F# G A G /

¹⁷ (E) C G A B C (D)(E)(D) C (D) G /

¹⁸ E F F# G A G / ¹⁹ E F F# G A G /

²⁰ G A B♭ B B B A F# D G /

²¹ E F F# G A G / ²² E F F# G A G /

²³ (E) C G A B C (D)(E)(D) C (D) C /

²⁴ G F# G C A C A C A G C (E)(G)(E) C G A C (E)(D) C /

# THE ENTERTAINER

## *The Entertainer*

Verse 3  ²⁵ **D D# E C E C E C** / ²⁶ **C** (D)(D#)(E) **C** (D)(E) **B** (D) **C** /

²⁷ **D D# E C E C E C** / ²⁸ **A G F# A C** (E)(D) **C A** (D) /

²⁹ **D D# E C E C E C** / ³⁰ **C** (D)(D#)(E) **C** (D)(E) **B** (D) **C** /

³¹ **C**(D)(E) **C**(D)(E) **C**(D) **C**(E) **C**(D)(E)

**C**(D) **C**(E)(D)(E) **B** (D) **C** / ₍bot₎**C** //

The difficulty with *The Entertainer* is getting hand speed on it. So again, we are going to have to do it very slowly: *two times slow, one time fast.* The quicker you can get it, the more chance you have of playing along with the CD. *The Entertainer* is a great tune to play, it involves a lot of talent, a lot of skill and when you can do this you know you have climbed that particular mountain. What we have done almost is like a pub sing-along version of it in a British style.

The fingering process in this, as usual, can be broken down and done as slowly as possible. You need to be right on

## CH 8 – THE CHROMATICS

top of your chromatic scale, there are some fairly unforgiving phrases going on. So again, do it slowly, run the tune in your head and concentrate.

Now the other thing to always think about with this one is there are some lovely runs across the bridge – you want to be about a note ahead of yourself to do it. So around the **B** and the **C** you are already crossing for the **(D)** in your mind. At phrase 7, you are crossing the bridge ten times. You are going to have bridge-crossing frenzy with that one.

So again, do this tune slowly, get it right, then have a go with the music. Now you have a go at being the entertainer and playing *The Entertainer*.

**61**
Chromatic Scale from bottom B♭ to top F♯ and back again

Play the full chromatic scale when warming up, slowly at first. It sounds colourful and will be very, very useful throughout your playing career. We will touch on this in the last chapter and thoroughly investigate its uses in the next volume of *Blowout Sax*.

# Ch 8 – Summary

This puts all the notes into an overall pattern, so you can visualise where all the notes live on the sax. Have a look at the overall pattern on the next page and see if you can work your breathing to its full capacity by blowing all 33 notes after one huge gulp.

Always work on the notes you have difficulty with. Make sure you can play any note, any time, anywhere because now it is time to start playing with the saxophone masters and the further exploration of your musicality will commence.

---

### Chapter 8
*The Chromatics*
**Summary**

We have learned:
- The colourful chromatic scale
- Finger twisting exercises
- Four show-stopping tunes

224

When you go **down**...

When you go **up**... the Sharps come **after** the Naturals

# Ch 8 – The Chromatics

# The Full Chromatic Scale

33/33

*the Sharps come before the Naturals*

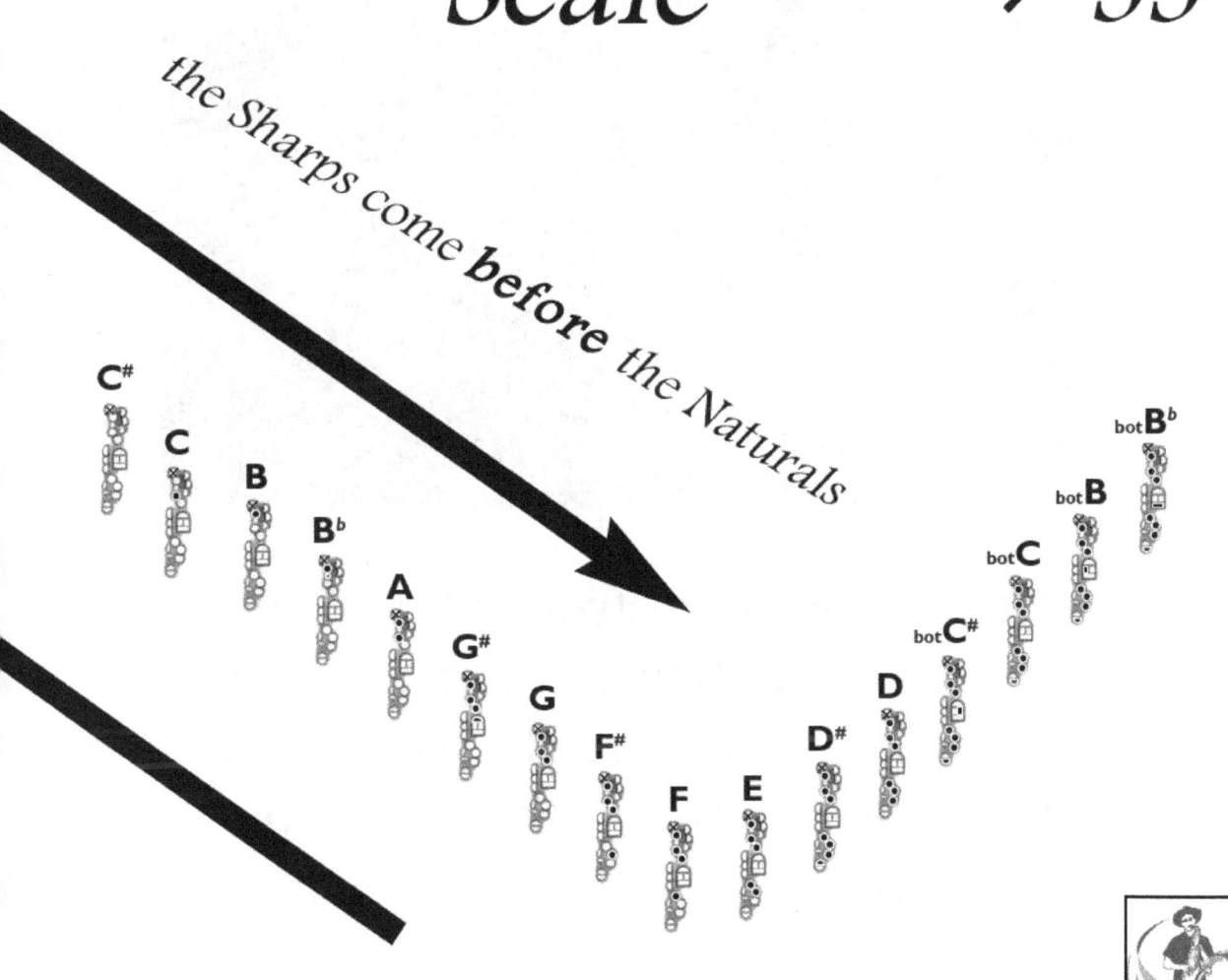

C#  C  B  B♭  A  G#  G  F#  F  E  D#  D  botC#  botC  botB  botB♭

"If you love an instrument that sings, play the saxophone. At best it is like the human voice... The challenge is to sing in that 'voice' that is outside your body."

Stan Getz, creator of 'The Beautiful Sound'.

## chapter nine

# The Finale Challenge

**B**y now you should be feeling very accomplished on your beloved saxophone. Your tone should be sweet and most of the 23 tunes should be feeling like they are *under your fingers*. Your inner ear is now awake and listening to music in a proactive way and this will help you become an even better player the longer you play.

The reason we have played through so many tunes is to build confidence and give you a firm foundation on the saxophone. The next stage will be to study many of the greats and having attuned your hearing you will be able to improve that much quicker.

Of the last two tunes, one is the quickest – yes, that's right, even speedier than *The Entertainer* – and that is *The Can Can*. The final tune of the book is the simple yet haunting melody of the most requested carol of all time, *In the Bleak Mid-winter*.

Both tunes will let you explore different aspects of playing 'the dream machine'.

CH 9 – 24TH TUNE

# The Can-Can

(Galop Infernal from *Orpheus in the Underworld*)
## Jacques Offenbach (1858)

Transport your imagination to the music halls of Paris in the 1890s when the high-kicking Can-Can was in full swing. In the times when it was easier to shock, colourful reputations were secured by women like 'La Goulue', the 'Queen of the Can-Can'. This 'ambassador of pleasure' would arrive leading a goat on a leash, go on stage and as she bowed low, she revealed an embroidered heart on the seat of her drawers.

When you are up to speed on this tune, pick a certain moment at a party when everyone is merry and we promise it will bring the house down! When you can kick your legs and play the tune on the saxophone like the fantastic Buster Bloodvessel from Bad Manners, then you know you've really cracked it.

# Ch 9 – 24th Tune

We know this works because our party band The Big Blowout have played it countless times to resounding effect. We even taught 35 students to work at it and then we played it live as a finale to one of our Blowout Sax School gigs.

In *The Can-Can* the music 'modulates', i.e. it moves from one set of notes to another – in this case, from **C major** (all the natural notes) to **G major** (all the naturals except **F#** instead of **F** (played in chapters 3 and 4).

# The Can-Can

This excellent piece of music is the ultimate finger-twister, so always remember the mantra for tricky phrases or passages of music:

## *"two times slow, one time fast"*

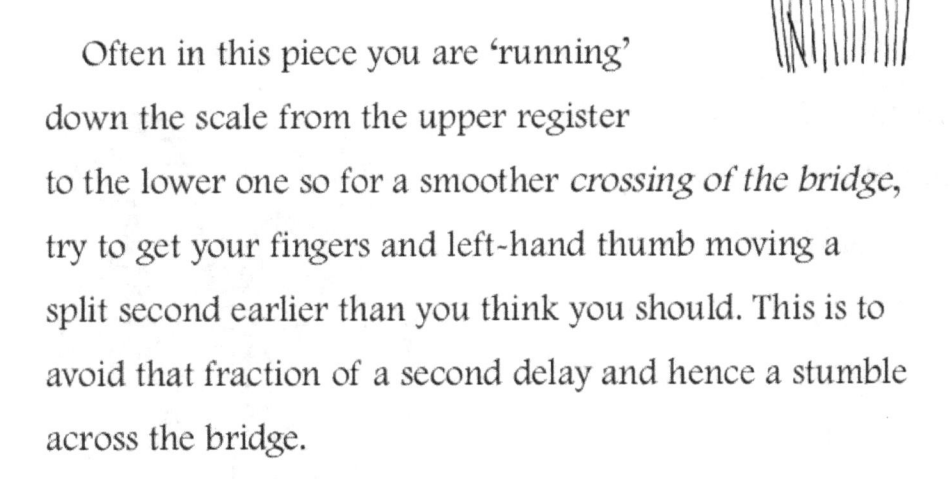

Often in this piece you are 'running' down the scale from the upper register to the lower one so for a smoother *crossing of the bridge*, try to get your fingers and left-hand thumb moving a split second earlier than you think you should. This is to avoid that fraction of a second delay and hence a stumble across the bridge.

As you become more intimate with the phrasing in each section you will be able to instinctively move your fingers to where they need to go. This will not only improve your hand speed but also lead to smooth bridge crossings every time.

The *Can-Can* is a tricky tune and even top professional saxophonists have to be *'on point'*, but that is one of the many joys of music – to be challenged in many different ways. The aim is to meet the challenges head-on and then you clearly feel, hear and see you are improving as a musician.

So take a deep, active breath and go for it. If you stumble, just keep going. This is one of those tunes where keeping up the momentum is more important than playing the tune precisely. In fact, that's true of a lot of live music – take on the challenge, have some fun and make your way through to the end.

# The Can-Can

## *The Can-Can*

**Main theme, verse 1**

bot**C D F E D G G G A E F D D D**

**F E D** bot**C C B A G F E D** bot**C /**

**D F E D G G G A E F D D D F**

**E D** bot**C G D E** bot**C /**

**Main theme, verse 2**

C D F E D G G A E F D D D /

F E D C C B A G F E D C

D F E D G G / G A E F D D D F

E D C G D E C /

**Middle 8**

**D A A B A G G / B C** E G E E D D /

E D D E D **G G A B A B A B A B A /**

**D A A B A G G / B C** E G E E D D /

E D D E D **G G A B A B A G/**

# 234

## CH 9 – 24TH TUNE

### *The Can-Can*

Verse 3   bot**C D F E D G G G A E F D D D**

**62**
With sax

**F E D** bot**C C B A G F E D** bot**C /**

**D F E D G G G A E F D D D F**

**63**
Without sax

**E D** bot**C G D E** bot**C /**

Verse 4   C D F E D G G G A E F D D D /

F E D C C B A G F E D C

D F E D G G / G A E F D D D F

E D C G D E C /

Middle 8   D A A B A G G B C E G E E D D /

E D D E D G G A B A B A B A B A /

D A A B A G G B C E G E E D D /

E D D E D G G A B A B A G /

# The Can-Can

**235**

## The Can-Can

Question and answer section

**B G E D / (D) A B C B A G /**

**B G E D / D D E F# A G G /**

**B G E D / (D) A B C B A G /**

**B G E D / D D E F# A G G /**

Middle 8

**D A A B A G G / B C (E)(G)(E)(E)(D)(D) /**

**(E)(D)(D)(E)(D) G G A B A B A B A B A /**

**D A A B A G G / B C (E)(G)(E)(E)(D)(D) /**

**(E)(D)(D) / (E)(D)(D) / (E)(D)(D) / (E)(D)(D)**

**(E)(D) x8 trills** gradually going faster and faster then modulating into **G major**.

Verse 5

**G A C B A (D)(D)(D)(E) B C A A A C B A G**

**G (F#)(E)(D) C B A G A C B A (D)(D) /**

**(D)(E) B C A A A C B A G (D) A B G /**

## Ch 9 – 24th Tune

### *The Can-Can*

Verse 6  G A C B A Ⓓ Ⓓ Ⓓ Ⓔ B C A A A C B A G

Ⓖ Ⓕ# Ⓔ Ⓓ C B A G A C B A Ⓓ Ⓓ /

Ⓓ Ⓔ B C A A A C B A G

Coda  Ⓖ Ⓕ# Ⓕ Ⓔ C Ⓓ Ⓓ G /

Ⓖ Ⓕ# Ⓕ Ⓔ C Ⓓ Ⓓ G /

Ⓖ Ⓕ# Ⓕ Ⓔ C Ⓓ Ⓓ /

Like peeling wedding bells.

Ⓖ Ⓕ# Ⓔ Ⓓ C B A G x8

CH 9 – 25TH TUNE

# In the Bleak Mid~Winter

'Cranham' melody by Gustav Holst (1906)
words by Christina Rosetti

This spine-tingling melody was set to a poem written by Christina Rosetti which had previously been published in a posthumous collection of *Poetic Works*. Holst's melody was based on a folk tune and it's simply beautiful – which is why it works so well.

Everyone has their own well of imagination and inspiration and rather than colour your thoughts with our experiences of this tune, draw on your own.

# Ch 9 – 25th Tune

This tune starts in **C major** and then changes into **A minor** halfway through. Learn the melody by heart so that it is *'under your fingers'* and you are able to play the notes with feeling.

With the intimacy of the phrasing you can personalise it by varying when you start on each phrase and the way you articulate it. Also, find the *keynotes* of each phrase and add or subtract notes like we did on *Amazing Grace*, while still singing the tune in your head so you know where you are.

Most of all, the challenge in this tune is to produce an inspired and captivating tone, which we will talk about in the next chapter.

# In the Bleak Mid-Winter 239

## In the Bleak Mid-Winter

Verse 1  In   the bleak mid-win-ter /  Fro-sty wind made moan /

(E) (F) (G) (E) (D) C / (D) (E) D   A   (D) /

Earth stood hard as   ir-on /  Wa-ter  like  a stone /

(E)   (F)  (G)(E)(D)C / (D)(E)D  C  C  /

Snow had  fal-len snow on snow /

(F)  (E) (F)(G)(A)(A)(E) /

Sn ~ o ~ w   on snow/

(G)(E)(D) C  B  /

In   the bleak mid-win-ter /

(E)(F) (G) (E) (D) C /

Lo ~ o ~ ong a-go

(D)(E)(D) C C  /

64  
With sax

65  
Without sax

Verse 2  
Our God, heaven cannot hold him  
Nor earth sustain;  
Heaven and earth shall flee away  
When he comes to reign:  
In the bleak mid-winter  
A stable-place sufficed  
The Lord Almighty  
Jesus Christ.

Verse 3  
Enough for him, whom cherubim  
Worship night and day,  
A breastful of milk,  
And a mangerful of hay;  
Enough for him, whom angels  
Fall down before,  
The ox and ass and camel  
Which adore.

# 240

CH 9 – 25TH TUNE

## *In the Bleak Mid-Winter*

Verse 4 Wh- at can I give him? / Po- or as I am /

(E) (F) (G) (E) (D) C / (D) (E) (D) (A) (D) /

If I were a shep-herd / I would bring a lamb /

(E) (F) (G) (E) (D) C / (D) (E) (D) C C /

If I were a wi- se man /

(F) (E) (F) (G) (A) (A) (E) /

I would do my part /

(G) (E) (D) C B /

Yet what can I give him? /

(E) (F) (G) (E) (D) C /

Gi- v- e my heart / Gi- v- e my heart /

(D) (E) (D) C C / (D) (E) (D) C C /

# Ch 9 – Summary

> **Chapter 9**
> *The Finale Challenge*
> **Summary**
> We have learned:
> • The art of running fast
> • Modulation
> • Two famous tunes

So, two contrasting tunes to finish the first stage of learning the saxophone the Blowout Sax way.

Make sure you have absorbed as many of the elements as you can from this book and in the final chapter – appropriately entitled 'You' – we will talk about the next exciting stages to explore on our beloved 'dream machine'.

"Music is your experience, your thoughts, your wisdom. If you don't live it, it won't come out of your horn. They teach you there's a boundary line to music. But man there's no boundary line to art." Charlie 'Bird' Parker.

## chapter ten

# You & Sax Mastery

**C**ongratulations to **You** for getting to this stage of playing the saxophone. This whole approach has been tailored to be about you. You are about to enter the next stage of your musicianship. This proven orginal approach will continue to help you play the saxophone in your own personal way.

# Ch 10 – You

Your foundation is firmly set. Your learning curve will continue to accelerate by playing and mixing with other enthusiastic musicians. You will continue to develop your own style throughout your saxophone career.

Now you must decide what you want to hear.

Your ultimate aim is that while you are playing, you are in a world of your own, with the saxophone being the instrument of your expression, and the *perfect dream* is as though the sax is playing itself.

To help create your own identity and your own tone you must choose from a number of options. There are many different styles of sax tone. You must decide what sort of voice will reflect your personality and to do this you must explore the great players.

# Ch 10 – Be Yourself

Every day you will be changing, developing and getting better. As you improve you may change your reeds, ideas, sax and influences and that is cool. Playing your sax is a continuous ongoing adventure.

Your tone, your message both emotional and spirtual, your style, your fluidity, your freedom of expression.
Be yourself.

# Ch 10 – Mouthpieces

At this stage it is well worth investigating changing your basic mouthpiece for a more professional and exciting one. This radical change should only be entertained when you have an idea of what sort of tone you want to achieve. Don't change it too early because your embouchure will not be settled enough to cope.

Every saxophonist expresses themselves through their voice and the mouthpiece is called the mouthpiece because it has a direct bearing on your sound.

There are many different types of sax tone – the smoky, sensual sound of Ben Webster's metal Otto Link, the beautiful sound of Stan Getz's ebonite Otto Link, the gut-bucketing, powerful, ripsnorting of Junior Walker's metal

# CH 10 – MOUTHPIECES

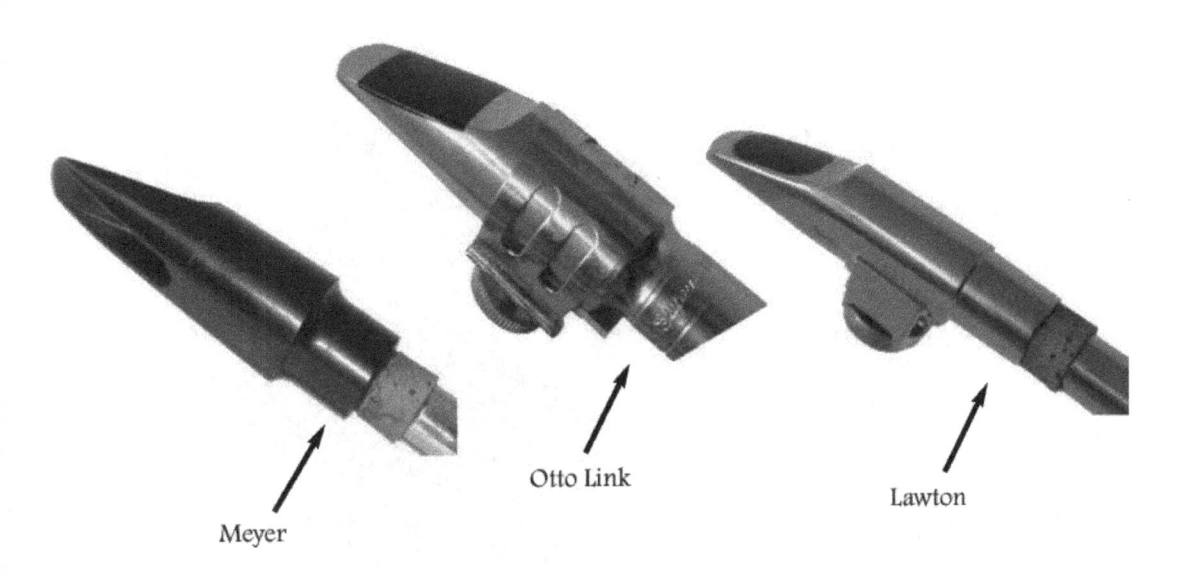

Meyer

Otto Link

Lawton

Lawton, or Lou Donaldson's bright, lighter, hard-rubber Meyer. All these mouthpieces we advocate and have sold at Blowout Sax and there are other types to try and experiment with.

If you find the metal weird on your teeth, use a rubber patch.

Reed wise, try different makes: Rico, Rico Royale and Vandoren Javas are very good and up to a 3½ thickness is usually enough to give you a big weighty sound.

Use a reed case, not just to keep favourite reeds in but different types of reed too – some reeds produce a thick, soft sound and others are more direct. It's always good to have a few reeds on the go. Remember to soak them before blowing them in.

# Ch 10 – Experiment

Go into a saxophone shop that has a big collection of mouthpieces. Experiment with all the different types available. Blow everything going in search of the sound that inspired you. Take your current favourite reed and take someone along who knows your playing, just to bounce ideas off.

Normally there is a spark and a bulb should appear over your head. That is the mouthpiece for you. Trust your intuition on this. If there's no spark, wait and really think about what you've learnt before trying again.

Think too about changing your ligature – there are now some excellent metal and leather ligatures which allow the reed to vibrate more freely. These are also excellent for improving Your Tone.

# Ch 10 – Love Your Saxophone

When you first get your all singing and dancing mouthpiece, take time to get your embouchure readjusted and make that tone beautiful.

Above all stay in love with your saxophone. Play whenever you can and look forward to climbing into your own world. Then it really is a course of what direction You want to take.

Next are all the scales you will need to get out there and play and the next set of books will show you why you need to learn them.

# BLOWOUT SAX SCALES CHART

Photocopy the tenor or alto scales chart on pages 254 and 255 and keep it in your case at all times.

We have played quite a few of these scales on our way to this point on the sax. Here are all the scales you will need if you are to play with other musicians and make your music.

'Con' in the columns on the left and right of the charts is short for 'concert pitch', which most other musical instruments, such as guitars and pianos, are played in.

# Blowout Sax Scales Chart

The left-hand 'con' applies exclusively to the major, so if the pianist is playing in **G major** you are in **A major** (tenor) and **E major** (alto). The right-hand 'con' applies strictly to the blues and minors. If, for example, the guitarist shouts out **F minor**, you can play either **G blues** or **G minor** (tenor) or **D blues** or **D minor** (alto).

The idea is that you can locate what notes you can use when you play with other musicians.

# Blowout Sax Scales Chart

As the great John Coltrane said: "I'm into scales right now..." Of the need to study and practise to continually realize his potential, he said:

"We have to keep on cleaning the mirror."

Learn these blues, majors and minor keys by heart and have them completely 'under your fingers'.
Then you have a set of keys to the kingdom of music.

# Blowout Sax Scales Chart – Tenor/Soprano

| Con. | Major (B♭ instrument) | Minor (Harmonic minor #7) | Minor Blues (blue note) | Con. |
|---|---|---|---|---|
| B♭ | C D E F G A B C | A B C D E F G A (G#) | A C D D# E G A | Gm |
| F | G A B C D E F# G | E F# G A B C D E (D#) | E G A B♭ B D E | Dm |
| C | D E F# G A B C# D | B C# D E F# G A B (B♭) | B D E F F# A B | Am |
| G | A B C# D E F# G# A | F# G# A B C# D E F# (F) | F# A B C C# E F# | Em |
| D | E F# G# A B C# D# E | C# D# E F# G# A B C# (C) | C# E F# G G# B C# | Bm |
| A | B C# D# E F# G# B♭ B | G# B♭ B C# D# E F# G# (G) | G# B C# D D# F# G# | F#m |
| E | F# G# B♭ B C# D# F F# | D# F F# G# B♭ B C# D# (D) | D# F G# A B♭ C# D# | C#m |
| B | C# D# F F# G# B♭ C C# | B♭ C C# D# F F# G# B♭ (A) | B♭ C# D# E F G# B♭ | G#m |
| F# | G# B♭ C C# D# F G G# | F G G# B♭ C C# D# F (E) | F G# B♭ B C D# F | D#m |
| C# | D# F G G# B♭ C D D# | C D D# F G G# B♭ C (B) | C D# F F# G B♭ C | B♭m |
| A♭ / G# | B♭ C D D# F G A B♭ | G A B♭ C D D# F G (F#) | G B♭ C C# D F G | Fm |
| E♭ / D# | F G A B♭ C D E F | D E F G A B♭ C D (C#) | D F G G# A C D | Cm |

# Blowout Sax Scales Chart – Alto

| Con. | Major (E♭ instrument) | Minor (Harmonic minor #7) | Minor Blues (blue note) | Con. |
|---|---|---|---|---|
| E♭ / D# | C D E F G A B C | A B C D E F G A (G#) | A C D D# E G A | Cm |
| B♭ | G A B C D E F# G | E F# G A B C D E (D#) | E G A B♭ B D E | Gm |
| F | D E F# G A B C# D | B C# D E F# G A B (B♭) | B D E F F# A B | Dm |
| C | A B C# D E F# G# A | F# G# A B C# D E F# (F) | F# A B C C# E F# | Am |
| G | E F# G# A B C# D# E | C# D# E F# G# A B C# (C) | C# E F# G G# B C# | Em |
| D | B C# D# E F# G# B♭ B | G# B♭ B C# D# E F# G# (G) | G# B C# D D# F# G# | Bm |
| A | F# G# B♭ B C# D# F F# | D# F F# G# B♭ B C# D# (D) | D# F# G# A B♭ C# D# | F#m |
| E | C# D# F F# G# B♭ C C# | B♭ C C# D# F F# G# B♭ (A) | B♭ C# D# E F G# B♭ | C#m |
| B | G# B♭ C C# D# F G G# | F G G# B♭ C C# D# F (E) | F G# B♭ B C D# F | G#m |
| F# | D# F G G# B♭ C D D# | C D D# F G G# B♭ C (B) | C D# F F G B♭ C | D#m |
| C# | B♭ C D D# F G A B♭ | G A B♭ C D D# F G (F#) | G B♭ C C# D F G | B♭m |
| A♭ / G# | F G A B♭ C D E F | D E F G A B♭ C D (C#) | D F G G# A C D | Fm |

# CH 10 – Blowout Sax Madmen

Now you have had a look at the scales. Here is The Blowout Sax road map to further saxophone mastery.

I have co-written several books which will help you learn more about the wonderful world of the saxophone. The first one, *Blowout Sax Madmen,* is an accessible, informative and visually entertaining guide to some of those larger than life characters who have wielded our favourite instrument.

Starting with Adolphe Sax and his own misadventures, we have selected 14 of the most interesting and flamboyant characters to have helped the development of the art of the saxophone.

## Ch 10 – Blowout Sax Madmen

# Ch 10 – Blowout Saxology

*Blowout Sax Madmen* is supplemented by *Blowout Saxology*, which captures the thoughts and wisdom of my twenty favourite saxophonists in the areas of soul, jazz, funk and pop.

This is enjoyable, invaluable and inspired learning. Listening to the great players, developing an ear for their distinctive styles and deciding what you like is an important part of becoming a musician.

Each tune has been transcribed in Blowout notation so that you can play with the Great and on your own. All in all it is a masterclass with musical legends – a great point of departure to help you find your own original voice.

# CH 10 – Improving Tone

To improve tone, the first logical stage is to study some of the finest sounds ever produced on the saxophone and with that in mind we have compiled a book called *Blowout Late Night and Spiritual Sax*.

*Blowout Late Night and Spiritual Sax* showcases the amazing variety of soulful saxophone performance. The book highlights the art of song interpretation, the craft of constructing aural soundscapes, the importance of memorable 'hooks', and the method of taking a phrase and reshaping it exquisitely.

All this is done through the medium of the saxophone's distinctive sound. In the art of playing the saxophone tone is everything. By concentrating on the element of sound and tone, the transcriptions and audio tracks in this book represent a vital and enjoyable resource for saxophone players.

All the tunes have been transcribed in Blowout notation. In addition the audio tracks provide a listening experience to reinforce the powerful performances of these great players. *Blowout Late Night and Spiritual Sax* provides an important bridge between the student and the top players to absorb the underpinning importance of a personal tone to the mastery of musical expression.

# CH 10 – BLOWOUT BLUE SAX

For us, the next step is to learn the blues as it is the basis of much great music. This we explore in *Blowout Blue Sax* with some inspirational performances from the very best blues players.

Here you'll find soul sax men King Curtis (seen below 'Walking the Bar') and Junior Walker, spine-tingling gospel tracks from Hank Crawford and Stanley Turrentine, some smokin' blues by Yuseef Lateef and some 60s grooves from Lou Donaldson and Eddie Harris.

Hearing, playing and absorbing those tunes will give you a deep grounding in where to go with your blues and a passport to the world of improvising your very own music.

# Ch 10 – Pop Sax

If you have come from the pop world, as I originally did, you may want to play *Blowout The Best Pop Sax Of All Time*, a collection of spine-tingling sax tunes, hooks, breaks and minatures. It's about finding what lights your fire – often it can be just a majestic couple of phrases which inspire you to take up the saxophone. All the classics are there . . . the ones that made me want to start playing.

The full transcript of *Baker Street*, the searing *Will You* solo, *Take 5*, all of the sublime sax on the Sadé songs, that wonderful sax break on Joan Armatrading's *Love and Affection* and Phil Woods' solo on Billy Joel's *Just The Way You Are* – these are some of the 'tingling' moments of saxophone magic captured in this book. Listening to the

# CH 10 – POP SAX

music and understanding why is a key part in becoming a great musician. All these 'choice cuts' lead you to want to play the 'dream machine' that is the saxophone and where you want to go.

The book has been laid out in different sections to give you as much insight as possible: the top five most requested pop solos; Great British hooks and miniatures; and Classic American pop solos.

Enjoy the brilliance of many of these unsung sax heroes. Some tunes you will know, some will be new to your ears. Marvel and be thrilled. Be inspired by playing them and learn as many outstanding musical traits as you can.

# Ch 10 – Sax Kings of Jamaica

For lovers of reggae ska music there is *Blowout The Kings of Jamaican Sax*. Here we introduce the world of the Jamaican Kings of the saxophone to those of you who want to play the very best inspirational ska and reggae tunes.

Being a 'rocker' at secondary school forced me to become a closet lover of two-tone ska in the late 70s and early 80s. Bands like Madness, The Specials and Bad Manners all featured saxmen playing leading roles in making the music 'happen'. The roots of this big two-tone sax sound were distinctly Jamaican. Although I didn't know it at the time, my favourite home-grown ska bands were indebted to some little-known reed masters from the Caribbean – the great Sax Kings of Jamaica who are the subject of this book. Our Kings of Jamaican Saxmen were so deeply involved in the creation of this new music that there is scarcely a ska hit that doesn't feature the saxophone.

Delving into the history of ska brought out surprise after surprise for me, the greatest of all being that many of these

# Ch 10 – Sax Kings of Jamaica

great musicians were mentored and inspired by a woman. And not just a woman but a saxophone-playing music teacher. And not just a music teacher but a nun – the legendary Sister Mary Ignatius Davies.

The legacy that Sister Ignatius has left in the playing of ska and reggae by these Kings of Jamaican Saxophone has made a massive impression on me, both as a player and teacher. These are some of the greatest discoveries in my musical life.

Why? Because this whole body of music is joyful, uplifting, and melodically infectious. It has its roots in masterful saxophone playing and is, above all, accessible to all.

# CH 10 – SAX KINGS OF JAMAICA

During the course of putting the book together I have trawled through countless recordings from each great saxophonist such as Tommy McCook, Roland Alphonso, Cedric 'IM' Brooks and Dean Fraser. I have cherry-picked great tunes, over 50 of them, and transcribed them by ear, and then lovingly notated them in our Blowout Sax tab style so that you can play and learn from these masters. Each tune is a magical pearl and the idea is to work to play those tunes that light your fire.

# Ch 10 – A Helping Hand

Covering all the books is well worth the effort as each player takes you on a different journey which helps you to become a versatile musician capable of any style. This depends on the journey and how far you want to go.

There are others too when you have advanced your techniques: *Blowout Kings of Soul Sax, Blowout Saxperimentalists, Blowout 60s SuperGroovy SoulSax Baby, Blowout Yakety Honkers, Swingers and Screaming Sax, Blowout Solo Sax* . . . and many others in the pipeline. You can get all these books from www.blowoutsax.com. So you have some interesting food for thought there.

To help you on your musical journey, on the next couple of pages is an instant guide to great sax – my rough, off-the-top-of-my-head top 20 tunes, balanced by those of Blowout Sax transatlantic jazzman, Craig Crofton.

# CH 10 – FAVOURITE TUNES

## Mark's top 20

1. *Children's World*, Maceo Parker
2. *Take 10*, Paul Desmond
3. *Alligator Boogaloo*, Lou Donaldson
4. *Bloodcount*, Stan Getz
5. *I Told Jesus*, Stanley Turrentine
6. *Pink Panther* (original version), Plas Johnson
7. *Soul Serenade*, King Curtis
8. *Can't Make You Love Me*, Candy Dulfer
9. *1974 Blues*, Eddie Harris
10. *Spanish Steps*, Van Morrison
11. *Angel Eyes*, Hank Crawford
12. *Baker Street*, Raf Ravenscroft
13. *A Whiter Shade of Pale* (Live at Fillmore), King Curtis
14. *Shotgun*, Junior Walker
15. *Brother Wind March*, Jan Garbarek
16. *I'm a Fool to Want You*, Dexter Gordon
17. *He of Zion*, Tommy McCook
18. *Jezebel*, Stuart Matthewman and Sadé
19. *I Ain't Got No Eye for Back*, Houston Preston
20. *Douala Serenade*, Manu Dibango

# CH 10 – FAVOURITE TUNES

## Craig's top 20

1. *Cosmic Rays,* Charlie Parker
2. *Parkers Mood,* Charlie Parker
3. *Giant Steps,* John Coltrane
4. *My Favorite Things,* John Coltrane
5. *Work Song,* Cannonball Adderley
6. *Jive Samba,* Cannonball Adderley
7. *Shake Everything You Got,* Maceo Parker
8. *Jacks Back,* Maceo Parker
9. *You'd Be So Nice to Come Home To,* Art Pepper
10. *Full House,* Johnny Griffin/Wes Montgomery
11. *Ruby My Dear,* Charlie Rouse/Thelonius Monk
12. *Rhythm-a-Ning,* Charlie Rouse/Thelonius Monk
13. *Freedom Jazz Dance,* Wayne Shorter & Miles Davis
14. *Footprints,* Wayne Shorter & Miles Davis
15. *E.S.P.,* Wayne Shorter & Miles Davis
16. *Olé,* Eric Dolphy/John Coltrane
17. *Shadow of Your Smile,* Dexter Gordon
18. *St Thomas,* Sonny Rollins
19. *Alfie,* Sonny Rollins
20. *Storm,* Stanley Turrentine

# Ch 10 – Your Journey

On this saxophone journey remember to find strength of character to overcome any attacks of confidence. You have to keep going. Sometimes you feel the learning curve seems to have stopped. Be patient because sometimes your playing is there, sometimes it's not. The hours you put in you **get back** with the sax.

# CH 10 – YOU

## My Freedom

*Artistic freedom is my freedom*

*I find my freedom within my limitations*

*I find my inner limitations and I surmount them*

*I push back the frontiers*

*I OPEN my SOUL*

*I am receptive to all ideas*

*To all influences*

*To beautiful instances*

*To hideous experiences*

*I experience all*

*I learn it all*

*I use it all*

*I control moods*

*I deliver feelings*

*And I find MY FREEDOM.*

*© Mark Archer 1998*

# We Did It

You can do anything in your life. I instigated 'The Big Blowout' when 529 saxophonists broke the world record for the largest saxophone ensemble in front of 25,000 people on the opening night of the Bath International Music Festival. Nearly 350 of the players were students at Blowout Sax.

**CERTIFICATE**

The largest saxophone ensemble is one of 529 musicians, who played, "Something Simple" by Archer/Scott and "Sunny Day" by Crofton for five minutes on 21 May, 2004 in Bath, Somerset, UK

Keeper of the Records
GUINNESS WORLD RECORDS LTD

# We Did It

273

# Bibliography

*Blowout Sax Madmen*, Mark Archer/Tony Clark

*Blowout Saxology*, Mark Archer/Stan Scott

*Blowout The Best Pop Sax Of All Time*, Mark Archer

*Blowout Blue Sax*, Mark Archer

*The Golden Age of Jazz*, William P. Gottlieb (Da Capo)

*The Sound of Jazz*, John Fordham (Hamlyn)

*Jazz*, Martin Lindsay (English Universtty Press)

*The Freedom Principle*, John Litweiler (Da Capo)

*The Jazz Handbook*, Barry McRae (Longman)

*The Decca Book of Jazz*, Peter Gammond (F. Mueller)

*The Jazz Book*, Joachim E Berendt (Paladin)

*As Serious as Your Life*, Valerie Wilmer (Pluto)

*The Song of the Hawk*, John Chilton (Quartet)

*Lester Young*, Lewis Porter (Smithsonian)

*Bird Lives*, Ross Russell (Quartet)

*Outcats*, Francis Davis (Oxford Uni. Press)

*Ornette Coleman*, Barry McRae (Apollo)

*Straight Life: Art Pepper*, Art & Laurie Pepper (Schirmer)

*Miles Davis*, Miles Davis & Quincy Troupe (Macmillan)

*Long Tall Dexter*, Stan Britt (Quartet)

# BIBLIOGRAPHY

*Sonny Rollins Programme*, Chip Stern

*Cleaning the Mirror*, Bill Shoemaker (Downbeat 1992)

*Master Blowers*, John Fordham (Guardian 1992)

*The Devil's Horn*, Michael Segell (Picador)

*Jazz Anecdotes*, Bill Crow (Oxford)

*The Music Quotation Book*, J & M Lindsay (Hale)

*Nowhere to Run*, Gerri Hirshey (Pan)

*Motown: The History*, Sharon Davis (Guinness)

*The Art of Saxophone*, Larry Teal

*100 Solos for the Saxophone*, Wise (Smet Pub.)

*Sax Studies*, Bill Bay (Mel Bay Pub.)

*Improvising Handbook*, Bill Bay (Mel Bay Pub.)

*Jazz Sax*, Charlie Gerard (Amcso)

*Rock Sax*, Pete Yellin (Amsco)

*Let's Play Jazz I, II & III*, Owen Brace (West Central)

*The Music Quotation Book*, Lindsay (Hale)

*The Styles of John Coltrane*, David Baker (CPP Belvin)

*Self Portrait of a Jazz Artist*, David Liebman (Dorn Publications)

*Developing a Personal Sax Sound*, David Liebman (Advance Music)

*Hello Mr Sax*, Jean-Marie Londex (Editions Musicales)

*Jazz Spoken Here*, Wayne Eustice/Paul Rubin (Da Capo)

*The Master Speaks*, Joe Allard (Video)

# CD Index

| CD 1 | | |
|---|---|---|
| 1 | C | 34 |
| 2 | B | 35 |
| 3 | C to B 'The Switch' | 36 |
| 4 | A | 37 |
| 5 | G | 38 |
| 6 | F | 45 |
| 7 | E | 46 |
| 8 | D | 47 |
| 9 | botC | 48 |
| 10 | C B A G F E D botC | 50 |
| 11 | botC D E F G A B C | 50 |
| 12 | (D) | 56 |
| 13 | (E) | 56 |
| 14 | (F) | 56 |
| 15 | (G) | 56 |
| 16 | (A) | 57 |
| 17 | (B) | 57 |
| 18 | (C) | 57 |
| 19 | (D)(E)(F)(G)(A)(B)(C) | 57 |
| 20 | 'T' Staccato on a C | 68 |
| 21 | C B A G F E D botC Staccato | 69 |
| 22 | C B A G F E D botC Legato | 70 |
| 23 | Swing feel tonguing every other note | 71 |
| 24 | Swing feel tonguing every 3rd note | 71 |
| 25 | Swing feel tonguing every 4th note | 71 |
| 26 | Swing feel tonguing every 5th note | 71 |
| 27 | Swing feel tonguing every 6th note | 71 |
| 28 | Slurring C B A G F E D botC | 71 |
| 29 | Crossing the Bridge C to (D) | 73 |
| 30 | *Camptown Races* slow with sax | 76 |
| 31 | *Camptown Races* slow without sax | 76 |
| 32 | C major C (D)(E)(F)(G)(A)(B)(C) | 78 |
| 33 | A minor A B C (D)(E)(F)(G)(A) | 79 |
| 34 | *Swing Low Sweet Chariot* with sax | 87 |
| 35 | *Swing Low Sweet Chariot* without sax | 87 |
| 36 | *When The Saints* verses 1 and 2 with sax | 89 |
| 37 | *When The Saints* verses 1 and 2 without sax | 89 |
| 38 | F# | 95 |
| 39 | (F#)(G) to (F#) trill | 96 |
| 40 | G major G A B C (D)(E)(F#)(G) plus arpeggio | 99 |
| 41 | Wah-Wahs (F#) | 101 |
| 42 | Wah-Wahs G | 101 |
| 43 | Woo-Woos (F#) | 102 |
| 44 | Vibrato (F#) | 103 |
| 45 | Varying the pulse slow to fast to slow | 104 |
| 46 | Foot tap | 104 |
| 47 | E minor E F# G A B C (D)(E) plus arpeggio | 107 |
| 48 | C# | 110 |

# CD Index

| | | |
|---|---|---|
| 49 | (C#) | 111 |
| 50 | C to C# (on) and off | 111 |
| 51 | D major D E F# G A B C# (D) plus arpeggio | 113 |
| 52 | B minor B C# (D)(E)(F#)(G)(A)(B) plus arpeggio | 113 |
| 53 | Glisses (D) to (C#) | 114 |
| 54 | B blues B (D)(E)(F)(F#)(A)(B) | 120 |
| 55 | St James Infirmary with sax | 122 |
| 56 | St James Infirmary without sax | 122 |
| 57 | Mourning Blues | 125 |
| 58 | Funky Growl | 126 |
| 59 | Buzz | 127 |
| 60 | Kicker | 128 |

**CD 2**

| | | |
|---|---|---|
| 1 | G# | 132 |
| 2 | G to G# | 133 |
| 3 | (G#) | 133 |
| 4 | A major A B C# (D)(E)(F#)(G#)(A) plus arpeggio | 134 |
| 5 | F# minor F# G# A B C# (D)(E)(F#) plus arpeggio | 134 |
| 6 | Brahms' Lullaby with sax | 135 |
| 7 | Brahms' Lullaby without sax | 135 |
| 8 | D#/E♭ | 136 |
| 9 | (D#)/(E♭) | 136 |
| 10 | (D#)/(E♭) trill to (D) | 137 |
| 11 | John Brown's Body with sax | 138 |
| 12 | John Brown's Body without sax | 138 |
| 13 | E major E F# G# A B C# (D#)(E) plus arpeggio | 139 |
| 14 | C# minor C# (D#)(E)(F#)(G#)(A)(B)(C#) plus arpeggio | 139 |
| 15 | B♭ | 140 |
| 16 | (B♭) | 141 |
| 17 | House of the Rising Sun with sax | 142 |
| 18 | House of the Rising Sun without sax | 142 |
| 19 | G blues G B♭ C C# (D)(F)(G) | 142 |
| 20 | botC | 152 |
| 21 | Camptown Races Cowboy version with sax | 155 |
| 22 | Camptown Races Cowboy version without sax | 155 |
| 23 | Pop Goes the Weasel | 157 |
| 24 | botC# | 162 |
| 25 | botB | 163 |
| 26 | St James Infirmary verse | 164 |
| 27 | botB♭ | 165 |
| 28 | Nobody Knows the Trouble I've Seen, with sax | 167 |
| 29 | Nobody Knows the Trouble I've Seen, without sax | 167 |
| 30 | botC#, botC, botB, botB♭ then botB♭, botB, botC, botC# | 169 |
| 31 | (topD) | 175 |
| 32 | (topD) to (C#) | 175 |
| 33 | (topD) to (C) | 175 |
| 34 | When the Saints using (topD), full version with sax | 180 |

# CD Index

| | | |
|---|---|---|
| 35 | *When the Saints* using (topD), full version without sax | 180 |
| 36 | (topD#) / (topEb) | 181 |
| 37 | (topE) | 182 |
| 38 | (topD) to (topD#) to (topE) | 182 |
| 39 | (topD) to (topE) | 183 |
| 40 | *Swing Low Sweet Chariot* using (topD) and (topE) | 184 |
| 41 | *Amazing Grace* with sax | 186 |
| 42 | *Amazing Grace* without sax | 186 |
| 43 | (topD) to (topF) with (topF#) at the end | 188 |
| 44 | D - D# - E | 202 |
| 45 | E - F - F# | 202 |
| 46 | D D# E F F# Up and down, right hand | 202 |
| 47 | G G# A | 202 |
| 48 | A Bb B | 202 |
| 49 | C C# (D) | 202 |
| 50 | F# G G# A Bb B C C# (D) Left hand | 202 |
| 51 | D D# E F F# G G# A Bb B C C# (D) Lower register | 203 |
| 52 | (D)(D#)(E)(F)(F#)(G)(G#)(A)(Bb)(B)(C)(C#)(D) Upper register | 203 |
| 53 | (D)(C#)(C)(B)(Bb)(A)(G#)(G) | 203 |
| 54 | (G)(F#)(F)(E)(D#)(D) | 206 |
| 55 | Top **D** to lower **D** in two gulps | 206 |
| 56 | Low **D** to top **D** in one gulp | 206 |
| 57 | Top **D** to low **D** in one gulp | 206 |
| 58 | F# blues F# A B C C# (E)(F#) | 208 |
| 59 | *The Entertainer* with sax | 220 |
| 60 | *The Entertainer* without sax | 220 |
| 61 | The full Chromatic Scale from botBb to (topF#) and from (topF#) back down to botBb | 222 |
| 62 | *The Can-Can* with sax | 234 |
| 63 | *The Can-Can* without sax | 234 |
| 64 | *In the Bleak Mid-Winter* with sax | 239 |
| 65 | *In the Bleak Mid-Winter* without sax | 239 |

## BLOWOUT SAX BOOKS

1 *The Blowout Teaching Book*
2 *Blowout Late Night and Spiritual Sax (AS/TS)*
3 *Blowout The Greatest Pop Sax (AS/TS)*
4 *Blowout Solo Sax (AS/TS)*
5 *Blowout Honkers Swingers and Screaming Sax (AS/TS)*
6 *Blowout Supergroovy 60's Sax Baby Yeah (AS/TS)*
7 *Blowout The King of SoulSax (AS/TS)*
8 *Blowout Blue Sax Part 1 (AS/TS)*
9 *Blowout Blue Sax Part 2 (AS/TS)*
10 *Blowout The Kings of Jamaican Sax (AS/TS)*
11 *Blowout The Saxperimentalists (AS/TS)*
12 *Blowout Smooth Sax Operators (AS/TS)*
13 *Blowout Tenor Sax Titans (TS)*
14 *Blowout The Pure the Beautiful and the Poet Of Sax (AS/TS)*
15 *Blowout The SoulSax Brothers (AS/TS)*
16 *Blowout The Pink Panther Sax Sound (TS)*
17 *Blowout Sax Epics (AS)*
18 *Blowout The Grandpappys of Boogaloo and Soul Makossa Sax (AS/TS)*
19 *Blowout Fat Funk Sax (AS/TS)*

OVER 450 TRANSPOSED TUNES
READY AS A SYLLABUS

plus
20 *Blowout Sax Madmen*
21 *Blowout Saxology*